# THE GREAT ALL-PICTURE
# CAT SHOW

# THE GREAT ALL-PICTURE
# CAT SHOW

ALEXANDRA ARTLEY

ASTRAGAL BOOKS · LONDON

First published in 1977 by Astragal Books, a division of
The Architectural Press Ltd, London

First paperback edition 1979

ISBN: 0 906525 15 2

Designed by Graham Mitchener

Composition by
Ronset Limited, Darwen, Lancashire

Printed in Great Britain by
BAS Printers Limited, Over Wallop, Hampshire

# Contents

# Acknowledgements

Many people have been generous with their time and personal possessions in the compiling of this book and I would particularly like to thank *Woman* magazine for help and encouragement; *Barbara Jones* who made her private collection available to me; *Bill Toomey* whose many hours of patient studio photography made the book possible; *Margaret Crowther* for staunch support in organising the cat portrait 'send-in' described in the Introduction; *Robert Melville* for many useful suggestions and the loan of one of his own paintings; *Eric Lister* of the Portal Gallery, London for making the works of several naive artists available to me; *Ann and Godfrey Golzen* who regularly raided their own collections on my behalf; *Bill Slack* who over the years has proved himself to have a telescopic eye for 'cat collectibles'; *Jan and Graham Mitchener* for ingenious design expertise; *Keith Kneebone* for his energetic production skills; *Philip Ward-Jackson* of the Courtauld Institute, London for locating the Puss In Boots frontispiece and *John Wilks* who first taught me about cats.

Since no cat book production team is complete without the feline friends who have given moral support over the years, I must also thank 'Mr Pussy' Golzen; 'Fluffy' Kneebone; 'Ginger' Sheppard; 'Mouseface' Crowther and 'Flora O'Hooligan' Artley who would all have typed the manuscript if they could.

**Photographs**

*Frontispiece:* The Courtauld Institute, London; *1, 2* page 2, *2* page 19: courtesy of Joy Robinson, The Warwick Doll Museum; *4* page 3, *15* page 17: courtesy of Kay Farquharson; *5, 6* pages 4–5: courtesy of Roger Sheppard; *11* page 13: courtesy of Bernard Scofield; pages 14–15, *3* page 36: courtesy of Martha Bush; *3* page 3 and *2* page 19: courtesy of Marion Waller, Keeper of Preston Manor and Rottingdean Grange, Brighton; *1* pages 20–21 The Bodleian Library, Oxford; *2* pages 20–21: a kind gift from Janet Pilch; *6* page 23: The National Magazine Company Limited; *4* page 37, *3* page 49, *5* pages 50–51, *9* page 116 and pages 70, 73, 77, 79, 80–81: The Victoria & Albert Museum, London; *5* page 38: kindly photographed by Cluny Gillies; *1* page 40: The Museum of Fine Arts, Boston, Massachusetts; *1* pages 44–45: courtesy of James Cartland and The Museum of Curiosities, Arundel; courtship line drawing, page 46: courtesy of Hilary Guise; *1* page 48: The American Museum In Britain, Bath; *4* page 49: The Art Gallery & Museum, Brighton; *1* page 54: courtesy of Mrs Philip Dalton; *2* page 55: The Newark Museum, Newark, New Jersey; *1, 2* page 58: Nick Barrington; *2* page 112: courtesy of The National Trust; *4* page 113: courtesy of The Crane Kalman Gallery, London; *7* page 115: courtesy of Ian McCallum; *15* page 119: photograph by Rick Bauer; *17, 18* pages 120–21, *30* page 127: courtesy of The Portal Gallery, London; *27* page 124: courtesy of Bruce Angrave; *29* page 126: by kind permission of E. Box.

**Text**

*An Irishman Sees The King Of The Cats* on pages 52–53
is reproduced by kind permission of Gill & Mac-
millan Limited, Dublin; *The Cat And The Mouse In
A Public House* on page 57 is reproduced courtesy of
The Blackstaff Press, Belfast and the three fairy
stories, *Puss In Boots, The White Cat* and *The History
Of Dick Whittington* on pages 71–83, 86–97 and 100–
109 have been reproduced in an abridged form by
kind permission of The British Library Board,
London. The information for the recipe *Apie And
Lapje's Dutch Dinner* on page 30 was kindly supplied
by Daphne de Wys , Amsterdam.

**Frontispiece**

This fine, swashbuckling statue of
Puss In Boots forms part of a monument
to Charles Perrault in the Tuileries
Gardens, Paris, done by the academic
French sculptor Gabriel Edouard
Baptiste Pech (1854–1930) in 1907.
Biographical details of Charles Perrault
and his connection with Puss In Boots
are given on page 68.
As *Puss In Boots* was first published in
1697, Pech has dressed the Master Cat
in his traditional costume as a 17th-
century *chevalier,* very much in the
manner of the dashing cavalier
D'Artagnan in *The Three Mouseketeers*.
When appearing in full fig, as here,
Puss In Boots usually wears a plumed
hat, a half cloak, turn-down boots and a
wide buckled belt, *plus* a necklace of
mice and a rat slung from his belt as a
pouch.
In this statue, Gabriel Pech has
consciously kept the details of Puss's
costume historically accurate, but this
practice has not usually been followed
by many other illustrators of the story,
who have generally modified the
costume, particularly the boots, to suit
the fashion of their own day. A very
interesting literary example of this
appears in the abridged poem given on
page 69. Published in 1811, this
satirical poem transforms Puss into a
fashion-conscious Regency buck who
orders his boots at Hoby's of St
James's, the fashionable London
bootmaker of Lord Byron and his circle

# Introduction

*D*ear Friends Of The Cat

Although it is very probable that I don't know you, the individual reader of this book, it is certain that we have one thing in common. We are both *aelurophiles* which means, according to very large dictionaries, that we are devotees of the domestic cat and that we collect or enjoy *almost* anything connected with its history, appreciation and welfare. As many writers have already pointed out, this fondness of ours for the cat defines us as a group which transcends regional and international barriers, much in the way that a love of music does, and if statistics are to be believed, the number of people who keep and enjoy the company of cats in Europe, the United States, Britain and Japan, has risen very dramatically in the past ten years or so. In other words, the fortunes of the domestic cat are once again in the ascendant after centuries of sometimes appalling cruelty, ignorance and indifference and with this new Golden Age in mind, I must now explain the various aims I hoped to achieve when compiling this book.

In the first place, I wanted to make *The Great All-Picture Cat Show* a happy book, a kind of celebration party for the current good fortune of the cat as a warmly appreciated member of the family circle. Because of this, I have not included any material about the cat deities of Ancient Egypt or the cruel persecution of cats as 'demons' by the medieval Church, but I have concentrated instead on the cat in a loving home environment. It seems that the Victorians, who put great emphasis on the importance of the home and family life, were the first people in modern history to rehabilitate the cat as a popular domestic personality. This is in contrast to the general post-medieval view of the cat as a purely utilitarian creature whose presence around the house was tolerated because of its usefulness in catching mice and rats. The Victorians were undoubtedly grateful for the cat's continued hunting abilities, but they also saw in the legendary maternal care and gentle discipline which a mother cat gives to her kittens, a perfect 19th-century image of ideal family behaviour in which a wise and beautiful mother gently but firmly brought up a large family of pretty and obedient children! An example of this can be seen in the sentimental paintings of Henriette Ronner (1821–1909) in which the activities of feline mothers and children are indistinguishable from those of their human counterparts (see 10, page 116).

As the Victorians invited the cat to join their family circle, I have tried to include as much 19th-century material in this book as possible, in honour of them. In the first part of the book, *Around The House,* I have also divided the illustrations into sections so that they hopefully represent, from dining-room, to smoking room, to garden, some of the divisions in a well-regulated Victorian home!

But, as I said earlier, I wanted *The Great All-Picture Cat Show* to be a kind of celebration party for the cat and no party is successful unless the guests enjoy participating in it. This, therefore, brings me to a word of explanation about the source of some illustrations which appear in this book. In January 1977 I was very grateful to be given the opportunity to make an announcement in a well-known magazine, inviting readers to send me portraits of their cats, whether paintings, drawings or needlework. People who love cats are frequently artists or craftsmen of one kind or another and I felt sure that hidden away in people's homes there must be many unknown works of art which other cat lovers would very much like to see. I was right. There was an overwhelming response to my announcement and although space restrictions in this book only permitted me to reproduce a small proportion of the works I received, the general standard of entries was very high. In this book captions marked with an asterisk [*] indicate that the accompanying illustrations are either the work or property of guest contributors to *The Great All-Picture Cat Show.* I would also like to take this opportunity to thank once again all those people who sent me art works for possible inclusion in the book and to say how sorry I am that we could not reproduce more. As many of them deserve to be seen by a wide audience perhaps in the future I will be given the opportunity to devote a whole book to the works of unknown or little-known cat artists.

In the meantime, fellow cat-lovers, here is *The Great All-Picture Cat Show* and I hope that in looking at its pictures and in reading its fairy-stories you get as much pleasure from the book as I had in compiling it.

Very best wishes

*Alexandra Artley*

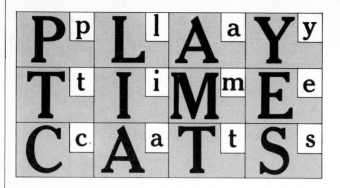

# PLAYTIME CATS

**1,2** Dating from *circa* 1905, this soft-toy mother cat with blue glass inset eyes and matching sleeping kitten has been beautifully preserved since its days in an Edwardian nursery

1

2

**3** Dating from the second half of the 19th century, this German wooden-based pull-along cat has a nodding head and inset wire whiskers

**4** This black mid 20th-century fur-fabric cat has a zip on the underside so that a child's night-dress can be stored in it during the day-time

**5,6** Front cover and plate from *Hey-diddle-diddle* a children's book published in 1882 with illustrations by Randolph Caldecott (1846–86). The cat and fiddle have been traditionally paired together in Europe since the Middle Ages, perhaps because both cat and violin were thought to be instruments of demoniac power

ONE SHILLING.

HEY DIDDLE DIDDLE and BABY BUNTING

R Caldecott's PICTURE BOOKS

GEORGE ROUTLEDGE & SONS

5

## The Fiddler Cat

*A cat came fiddling out of a barn*
*With a pair of bagpipes under her arm.*
*All she could play was diddle-dum-dee,*
*The mouse shall marry the bumble bee.*
*Play cat, dance mouse,*
*We'll have a wedding in our good house.*

TRADITIONAL

6

*A Riddle*

In almost every house I'm seen,
   (No wonder then I'm common,)
I'm neither man, nor maid, nor child,
   Nor yet a married woman.

I'm pennyless, and poor as Job,
   Yet such my pride by nature,
I always wear a kingly robe,
   Though a dependent creature.

*Question:* *What*

*Based on* THE AMUSING RIDDLE BOOK Montrose 1845

*m I?*

Answer: *A Cat*

## The Fairy Cat

The Fairy Queen has a Fairy Cat
  With a coat of bluish grey,
And a fairy has to comb it out
  And brush it every day.

The fairies all share the combing
  And they're usually in the wars,
For Lulu, although a fairy cat,
  Has very unfairy claws!

*Cat Gossip* No 39, 31 August 1927

**7** Late 19th-century scrap showing a long-hair cat, with a blue satin bow round its neck, sitting in a basket. These small coloured cut-outs were bought for children to paste into scrap-books

## The Minister's Cat

The Minister's Cat was a popular late 19th-century fireside game which, like many Victorian children's games, had a useful educational purpose behind it. In this case, the underlying object was to increase the vocabulary of the young participants in the nicest possible way! The game was played alphabetically. The first player began by saying, 'The minister's cat' is 'an ambitious cat'; the next player might say 'an arrogant cat' and the third might continue with 'an apologetic cat' and so on round the circle of children until all had named an attribute beginning with A. The next round of descriptions to be supplied began with B, then C, until the whole of the alphabet had been worked through. When a child failed to supply a description of the minister's cat he would drop out of the game, ultimately leaving a winner. Adults who play this game generally find it very easy to describe the minister's cat until they reach the letter X.

LITTLE JACK HORNER.

*A Happy Christmas to you.*

Jack the Giant Killer.

**8,9** Two illustrations from Louis
Wain's nursery-rhyme postcard series
in which cats play the part of other
fairy-tale characters, here, Little Jack
Horner and Jack The Giant Killer.
Louis William Wain (1860–1939) was
an immensely popular humorous cat
illustrator who taught art at the West
London School of Art from 1881–82,
before joining the staff of *The Illustrated
Sporting and Dramatic News* in 1882 and
*The Illustrated London News* in 1886.
Prolific in output as a magazine
illustrator, one of his most successful
ventures was *The Louis Wain Annual*
which first appeared in 1901. Wain
visted New York from 1907–10 and
while there produced two series of strip
cartoons called *Cats About Town* and
*Grimalkin.* In 1917 he was offered the
opportunity to make a cartoon film
called *Pussyfoot* which he subsequently
abandoned. Louis Wain entered a
private mental home in 1925 and his
late work, apart from its own intrinsic
merit, forms a classic visual study of the
onset of schizophrenia. Other examples
of this artist's work may be found on
pages 63 and 118—119

# Cat's Cradle

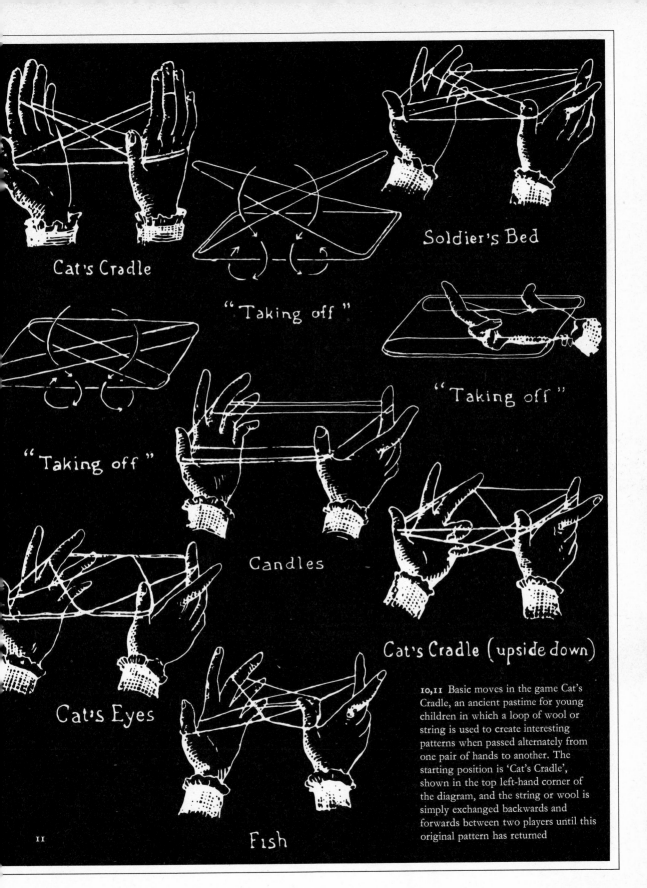

Cat's Cradle

"Taking off"

Soldier's Bed

"Taking off"

"Taking off"

Candles

Cat's Cradle (upside down)

Cat's Eyes

Fish

10,11 Basic moves in the game Cat's Cradle, an ancient pastime for young children in which a loop of wool or string is used to create interesting patterns when passed alternately from one pair of hands to another. The starting position is 'Cat's Cradle', shown in the top left-hand corner of the diagram, and the string or wool is simply exchanged backwards and forwards between two players until this original pattern has returned

11

Great A, little a,
  Bouncing B;
The cat's in the cupboard,
  And she can't see.

Pussy-Cat sits by the fire;
    How can she be fair?
In walks the little dog;
    Says: "Pussy, are you there?
How do you do, Mistress Pussy?
    Mistress Pussy, how d'ye do?"
"I thank you kindly, little dog,
    I fare as well as you!"

**12,13** Two illustrations by Frederick Richardson from an American collection of nursery-rhymes entitled *Mother Goose,* published in Chicago and New York in 1915

**14** Cover of a late 20th-century children's 'squeaky' book manufactured in Belgium, depicting a long-hair kitten with a blue satin bow round its neck. When the medallion on the kitten's chest is pressed, it emits a plaintively drawn-out 'miau'

14

## A Poem About The Origin Of The Manx Cat

Noah, sailing o'er the seas,
  Ran fast aground on Ararat,
His dog then made a spring, and took
  The tail from off a pretty cat:
Puss through the window quick did fly,
  And bravely through the waters swam,
Nor ever stopped, till, high and dry,
  She landed on the Calf of Man.
Thus tailless puss earnt Mona's thanks,
  And ever after was called Manx.

*Cat Gossip* No 33, 20 July 1927

**15** Late 20th-century white long-hair toy kitten with inset glass eyes probably manufactured in Hong Kong. The toy seems to be covered in rabbit fur on a composite base and the shaft of the tail is wire so that it can be adjusted to a variety of positions

15

# Tea Time Cats

If you see a cat shape in the tea-leaves of your cup you must beware, for it reveals the presence of secret enemies.

*The Fortune-Telling Tea-Cup: Wonderful Combinations In The Tea Leaves* New York 1899

## A Wise Cat's Guide To The Gentlemen Its Mistress Entertains To Tea

*While pouring to a gentleman*
*And whispering soft, 'How much?'*
*Of sugar or of cream he'll have*
*You may discover such*
*As what his qualities may be,*
*If cruel or if kind,*
*And if a partner suitable*
*For life in him she'll find.*

Tea with much cream and sugar · INCLINED TO BE EXTRAVAGANT
Tea with much cream and no sugar · GENTLE AND AFFECTIONATE
Tea with little cream · INDEPENDENT AND RESOLUTE
Tea with no cream but some sugar · CAREFUL AND THRIFTY
Sweet tea · VIVACIOUS AND CLEVER
Tea with little sugar · IMPULSIVE AND KIND-HEARTED
Tea with no sugar · THOUGHTFUL AND CONSTANT
Tea without either · NEAT AND TIDY, INCLINED TO BE FADDISH
Strong tea · ACTIVE AND DETERMINED
Weak tea · GENTLE AND TOLERANT
Easily suited · A CAREFREE HUSBAND
No tea · ECCENTRIC AND IMPRUDENT

*Tea-Cup Reading: Your Fate In Your Tea Cup* London 1907

I

**1** This handsome black earthenware tea-pot in the shape of a cat was manufactured in England during the 1920s. The raised fore-legs form the spout, the looped tail a handle and the cat's head, which is the tea-pot lid, can be swivelled to look in any direction

**2** Late 19th-century child's cotton handkerchief printed with scenes from a cats' tea-party at which Miss Tabbi entertains Mr Velvet Purr, Miss Tortiseshell, Miss Kitty and a solicitor and his client. At the end of the afternoon, Sir Claud Scratch and Captain Black quarrel in the street

**3** Dating from *circa* 1925, this child's earthenware tea-set is decorated with transfer prints of Felix the Cat, a cartoon-film character invented by an Australian, Pat O'Sullivan, in 1922. The captions on the tea-set read: 'Felix Takes A Walk'; 'Please Felix Don't Shoot'; 'Now Felix Keep On Walking' and 'Will You Walk With Felix?'

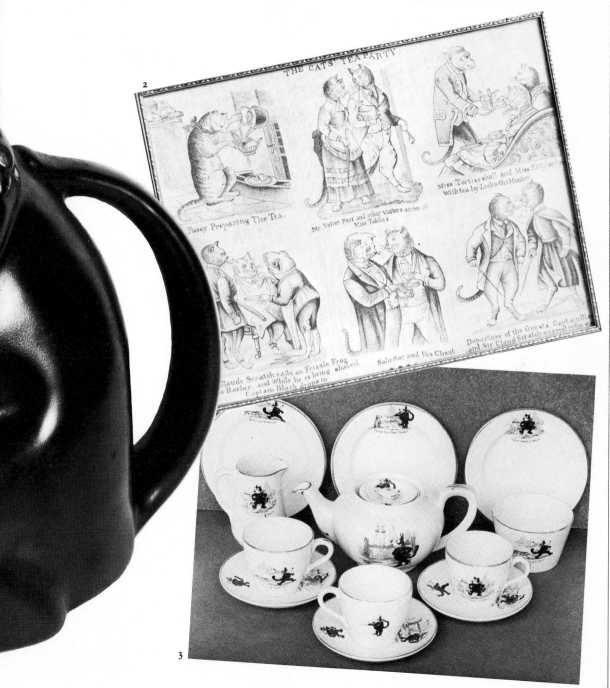

1 Dating from *circa* 1884, this British Victorian windowbill advertisement shows three cats nonchalantly watching a bull-dog straining at a leash which is made from one miraculous strand of J. & P. Coats' sewing cotton

2 Belgian black velvet cat and rat with green glass eyes and gold-coloured machine-finished edging, probably intended for the *appliqué* decoration of a woman's dress, coat or jacket during the 1920s

# Needlework Cats

**3** Mid 19th-century French pin-cushion made of white porcelain in the shape of a cat's head

**4** Head of a Persian cat embroidered in dark brown silk on cream linen by Mrs William Buckley *

**5** Portrait head of her Siamese cat, Sam, embroidered in cream, chocolate brown and blue silks on a black cotton background by Miss Vicki Moule

**6** *The Cat Sat On The Mat*, a tapestry designed in 1976 by Heather Clarke

3

4

5

**7** Panel of Edwardian crotchet work with a repeated motif of a kitten chasing a ball, reproduced by courtesy of Miss M. Ashford *

**8** Entitled *Royal Pride*, this tapestry by Amanda Lowe, aged twelve, was inspired by the story of a Siamese Prince and Princess who, because of their great vanity, were turned into cats and set to perpetually guard a vase *

**9** Portrait of *Tiger* embroidered on green cotton by Mrs M. Jackson *

**10** In this embroidery by Prue Johnson of a cat reclining on a door mat, the caps of the milk bottles are worked in silver thread *

7

8

9

10

P. JOHNSON

**11** *Look Out Church Mice, Here I Come!*
an embroidery worked on linen by
Miss Carol Preston who used her own
cat *Sooty* as a model. This embroidery
is reproduced by courtesy of Mrs
Vera Preston *

**12** Portrait of *Dicky* sleeping, an
embroidery worked in tabby colours
on white cotton by Felicity Norton *   **11**

**12**

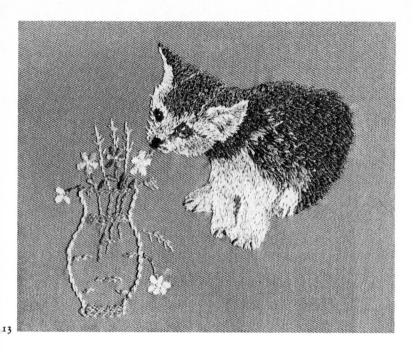

**13**

**13** Portrait of a cat delicately sniffing a flower, embroidered on green cotton by Miss E. Ritchie *

**14** The design of this realistic 'tabby' cushion, printed on cotton cloth, originally came from the Arnold Print Works, North Adams, Massachusetts, where it was patented in 1892

**14**

## St Agatha The Cat Saint

### FEBRUARY 5th

Saint Agatha, who was martyred on 5th February AD 251, was believed in the Languedoc area of southern France to take the form of a cat to punish women who did such household work as spinning, washing or baking on her day. In the Languedoc dialect her name was misconstrued to 'Santo Gato'. As Saint Agatha was the Protectress against fire, lightning and hail, one means of banishing her in cat form was apparently to shout, 'The cemetery is on fire!' whereupon she would flee back to her grave. Two folk tales illustrating this belief are given in this section.

1 Young female cat being tempted on a roof between good and evil, an illustration by the early 19th-century French artist 'Grandville' from his book *Scènes de la Vie Privée et Publique des Animaux* published in Paris in 1842. Further biographical information about Grandville is given on page 92

## St Gertrude Of Nivelles

### MARCH 17th

St Gertrude, who was born in AD 626 and died at an unverifiable date between AD 653–59, became Abbess of the double monastery of Nivelles, Belgium in AD 652. This saint was sometimes portrayed accompanied by a cat because she was specially invoked against plagues of mice and rats. An instance of this occurred as late as 1822 when, in response to a plague of field-mice in the agricultural areas of the Lower Rhine, a group of peasants congregated at a shrine of St Gertrude in Cologne to make her an offering in the form of gold and silver mice. St Gertrude's cat-like struggle against mice is also illustrated by a legend which explains how, when the saint was spinning, the Devil used to visit her in the form of a mouse to gnaw through her thread and thus attempt to provoke her to anger.

## The Cat Saint And The Baker Of Bread

Here, in the Soule, the mistress of the house was baking bread on St Agatha's Day when a cat came in and snatched a piece of dough. 'Get out of here, cat!' cried the woman to which the animal replied, 'I am no cat but Saint Agatha and you are baking bread on my day. Look up.' The woman then looked up and saw that for her irreverence the house was afire.

Based on Violet Alford 'The Cat Saint' *Folk-Lore* Vol LII, No 3, September 1941

# Cat Saints

## St Ivo Hélory
### MAY 19th

St Ivo Hélory, or St Ives as he is sometimes better known, was born at Treguier, Britanny in 1253. From his youth as a law student in Orléans to his death in 1303 he was noted for his austere life as an ascetic and for his kindly and impartial administration of justice. Although poor by choice himself, he never accepted bribes and by championing the cause of the poor and helpless he became known as The Poor Man's Advocate. As the patron saint of lawyers, St Ivo is often portrayed accompanied by a cat. In this context the cat was said to represent the cunning, greed and duplicity of the medieval legal profession, characteristics which St Ivo totally rejected in his own administration of justice.

## The Cat Saint And The Washerwoman

A woman announced that she was going to begin washing but her neighbour reminded her it was St Agatha's Day and that this work was forbidden. The woman impatiently cried, '*Santo Gato gatera e la ruscado se fara*!' or, 'Saint Cat shall kitten and I shall have my wash!' She began her wash and immediately 'a sort of cat' appeared at the chimney corner. This creature cried, 'Empty it! Empty it!' every time the cauldron had to be emptied in the course of the wash.
The terrified woman ran to her wise neighbour. She was told she must go to the window when it was time to empty the last cauldron and to cry out, 'The cemetery is on fire!' Whereupon the cat howled, '*Al miu oustalou*!' or, 'To my little home!' and fled.

## St Verena Of Zurzach
### SEPTEMBER 1st

St Verena of Zurzach, whose biographical dates are unknown, is venerated throughout Switzerland as a harvest saint. In illustrations she is usually accompanied by ears of corn and a cat, symbols of her fertility-giving powers, and she is especially invoked by childless married couples and by girls about to be married, who leave their maiden head-dresses in front of St Verena's statue before their wedding.
St Verena ended her days in a cell built for her at Zurzach where her tomb shows her holding a comb and bowl, emblems of her charitable work amongst the peasants, in whose personal cleanliness she was particularly interested.

## Cats And Corpses

It is a common remark that a cat will not settle in a house with an unburied corpse. I know not how far the truth of this saw may extend; but this I do know, that on the decease of the writer's maternal parent, the house cat left the dwelling and took to the garden; where, by scratching the earth, she made herself a kind of lair and extended herself therein like a hare in her form, with her nose partially covered with loose soil. This I noticed on many occasions during the period the body was uninterred.

Michael A. Denham *Folk-Lore: Or, Manners, Customs, Weather Proverbs, Popular Charms, Juvenile Rhymes etc in the North of England* Richmond, Yorkshire 1852

# CATS AT BREAKFAST AND DINNER

## Breakfast Marmalade

*Marmalade cats are jolly and super:*
*They should be called Keiller, John Peel or Frank Cooper.*
*They slip out with the empties, return with the post,*
*As breakfast companions they're perfect with toast.*

## Apie And Lapje's Dutch Dinner

$\frac{1}{2}$ lb ox heart
1 medium-sized carrot
A few sprigs of parsley
2 oz cabbage
1 slice of stale brown bread
$\frac{1}{2}$ pint of stock made from a bouillon cube *or* $\frac{1}{2}$ pint of water plus $\frac{1}{4}$ teaspoonful of salt

Apie and Lapje are two handsome cats happily resident in Amsterdam, who have yoghurt with wholemeal breadcrumbs crumbled into it for breakfast and this favourite recipe for dinner. It should be said, however, that mature adult cats will usually only eat vegetables if a small quantity was first introduced into their diet as kittens. This is what happened with Apie and Lapje. 'Apie' means 'monkey' and 'Lapje' means 'patchwork.'
Cut up the ox heart into half-inch pieces, together with any tough interior tubes which may be present. Chop up all the vegetables and parsley finely and put both the heart and vegetables in a pan, covering them with the stock and then bringing them to the boil. Reduce the heat and simmer gently until the vegetables are very soft. Remove the pan from the heat and while it is standing to cool, break up the stale brown bread and put it to soak in the liquid surrounding the vegetables and meat. Allow this mixture to cool to room temperature before serving it to your cat. Please remember it is cruel to give hungry animals food which is either steaming hot or straight from the freezer.

## A Recipe For Substitute Cats' Milk

2 tablespoonfuls of condensed milk
2 tablespoonfuls of boiled water
$\frac{1}{4}$ teaspoonful of corn syrup
$\frac{1}{4}$ teaspoonful of Bovril, Marmite or a similar yeast-based bouillon concentrate

Occasionally, cat owners are faced with an emergency when they find an abandoned unweaned kitten or their own queen dies after littering, leaving behind a band of hungry orphaned kittens. Veterinary analysis has shown cats' milk to be very rich and this recipe sets out to simulate that richness. Commercially marketed dried cats' milk substitutes are available, of course, but emergencies rarely choose to happen

1 *Their Morning Meal,* an early illustration by the popular late 19th-century cat illustrator, Louis Wain. A biographical note about this artist may be found on page 11

## Beef Chasseur: A Hunting Game

3 or 4 oz of cheap but bloody stewing meat
4 or 5 feet of clean string
A narrow and sharply pointed skewer

This recipe is not so much a meal but a game and the main ingredient is not food at all, but a suitably large and easily-cleaned floor, or preferably a garden, in which to run about.

Cut the meat into half-inch cubes and pierce each cube with the skewer. Tie a large secure knot at one end of the string and then thread the other end of the string through the hole in a cube of meat. Then, trail the cubes on the string across the floor or the garden while your cat chases, 'kills' and finally eats them. This food game is particularly useful for cat owners who wish to induce the hunting instinct in cats which are slow to catch mice, but do be careful in your supervision of the string. If, by misfortune, your cat should eat the string and it later appears at the anus, *do not pull it* but seek veterinary advice immediately.

Cat lovers need not be reminded that if too long a time elapses between the chasing and the actual 'killing' and eating in this game, it does not become an exciting pastime for your cat, but a rather refined torment.

when the shops are open for one to buy them!

Mix the syrup and the bouillon concentrate in a cup with a little of the condensed milk and then gradually add the remaining ingredients, noting that the recipe says 'boiled' and *not* 'boiling' water. When the ingredients are thoroughly blended, stand the covered cup in a basin of boiling water to bring the substitute milk up to lukewarm, kitten-body temperature and then decant small quantities of it into a suitable feeding vessel. Tiny, kitten feeding-bottles are available from large, well-stocked pet stores, but in an emergency a *clean* fountain-pen filler, a drinking straw used like a pipette or even the corner of an absorbent towel, are better than nothing. Do not expect a very young kitten to drink gallons of this substitute milk at one go, as the stomach of a newly-born kitten is only the size of a walnut.

## May Kittens and Mousing

Kittens born in May are even still proverbially spoken of and looked upon as *bad mousers*. I only within the present year heard a female say that 'She wad nivver mair keep a May Kittling as lang as she lived, for they were just good for nought at all!'

Michael A. Denham *Folk-Lore: Or, Manners, Customs, Weather Proverbs, Popular Charms, Juvenile Rhymes etc In The North Of England* Richmond, Yorkshire 1852

## Cats Who Bait Mouseholes

I recently read of a cat that ate cheese and then breathed down a mousehole, and it may interest some of your readers to know that I have seen two of my neuter cats bait a mousehole. On one occasion I was in the cellar getting some meat out of the pantry, when I noticed my brown tabby neuter begging beside me, so I threw him a little piece of meat, and was surprised to see him push it along the floor with his paw for some distance, and then place it exactly above a mousehole by the wall. He then retired to a distance of about two yards, and sat watching it all the evening! Another time, when in the kitchen, my silver tabby neuter was given a little piece of pudding, which he did not eat, but pushed along the floor to a mousehole by the kitchen stove just as the other cat had done, and then watched it for some time; becoming tired of this he ran out into the garden, and in the meantime the brown tabby came along, and seeing the piece of pudding ate it up! Soon the silver tabby returned from the garden, and went straight to the mousehole, only to find that his bait had disappeared; he could not make it out at all, and put his paw right down the hole, then withdrew it, covering the hole over again with his paw in case the mouse should escape!

From *Cat Gossip* No 8, 26 January 1927

**2** Cats standing on each other's shoulders to steal mouse jam from a cupboard, a cartoon strip by Louis Wain which appeared in *The Boy's Own Paper* in 1901

Pussy's Breakfast

# CATS IN THE GARDEN

## An Ancient Herbal Remedy To Prevent Cats Catching Domestic Fowls

To keep Cats from hunting of Hens, they use to
tie a little wilde Rew under their wings, and so
likewise from Dove-coates, if they set it in the
windowes, they dare not approach unto it for
some secret in nature.

This quotation comes from Edward Topsell's
book *The History Of Four-Footed Beasts And
Serpents Describing At Large Their True and Lively
Figure* published in London in 1658. If, as he says,
cats are naturally averse to the herb rue, the
planting of it might be a gentle and natural way
of dissuading strange cats from certain parts of
one's garden, particularly if this planting plan
were reinforced elsewhere with a bed of cat-mint
which cats love. Similarly, a bunch of rue tied
to the bars of budgerigar's or canary's cage
might protect caged birds from feline assaults
during their owner's absence!

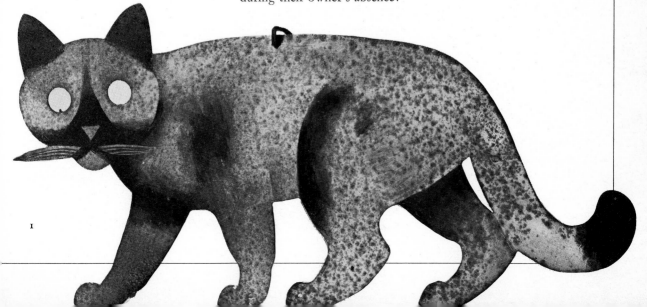

I like little pussy, her coat is so warm,
And if I don't hurt her she'll do me no harm;
So I'll not pull her tail, nor drive her away,
But pussy and I very gently will play.

**1** This 20th-century French metal bird-scarer in the shape of a stalking cat has been attractively painted by its present owner. Originally, the bird-scarer would have been suspended by a string, passed through the loop on its back, to a stake or sturdy plant so that it could swing freely in the breeze and frighten away birds. The sockets in the head of this example are now empty, but as in the two British bird-scarers which follow, they would originally have held glass eyes

**2** Two 20th-century British metal bird-scarers in the shape of cats' heads, painted black to protect them against weathering. The nose, mouth and whiskers of each cat have been stamped out of the metal and the eye sockets hold glass marble-like eyes which are alarmingly realistic when seen directly against bright sun-light

**3** Illustration by Frederick Richardson from an American collection of nursery-rhymes entitled *Mother Goose* published in Chicago and New York in 1915. The well-known children's poem, of which the first verse is given here, was originally written by the London-born children's writer Jane Taylor (1783–1824) who, in conjunction with her sister Ann, published it in their highly successful *Original Poems For Infant Minds* in 1804. Another well-known poem by Jane Taylor is 'Twinkle, twinkle little star', which first appeared in *Limed Twigs To Catch Young Birds* in 1808

**4** English mid 18th-century soft-paste porcelain figure of a cat up a tree brightly painted in enamel colours

4

5

**5** Late 20th-century English ceramic cat permanently engaged in an assault course on the fanlight of a house in Sussex, England

**6** Portrait of *Nicky* seated in a flower garden, painted in oil on a circular board by Maggie Brooks *

**7** Mounted on red cardboard, this cat's head was made by Mrs Nell Sharp from pressed white flowers, with yellow buttercups for eyes and dried grasses for whiskers *

1 This starkly simple painting of an enigmatic black cat was painted by an American doctor, Andrew L. von Wittkamp M.D., about whom little is known except his name and this painting which was probably done *circa* 1855 in Philadelphia

# BLACK CATS

## I Like Black Cats Because

· They are discreetly dressed for every occasion
· They bring good luck to their owners
· If wearing a white bow tie they make excellent butlers
· They are dramatic by day and invisible by night
· They make unwelcome visitors feel ill at ease by
suddenly looking sinister
· The black leather on their paws and nose is always in
good taste and very durable
· They enjoy Hallow'een parties
· Their pleasing sobriety of manner fits them for
unobtrusive duties in undertakers' parlours, public
libraries, ladies' waiting rooms and the better kind of
family restaurant
· When they stretch their fore-paws they appear to be
wearing long black elbow-length evening gloves
· They are used to riding pillion when I fly across the
sky at night

## Some European Superstitions About Black Cats

In Russia the people commonly believe that black cats
become devils at the end of seven years. In parts of
Southern Europe they are held to be serving as
apprentices to witches. In Brittany there is a dreadful
tale of black cats that dance with unholy glee around
the Cross, and the Sicilian peasant is sure that if a
black cat lives with seven masters, the soul of the
seventh will accompany him back to the infernal regions.

Cat Gossip No 18, 6 April 1927

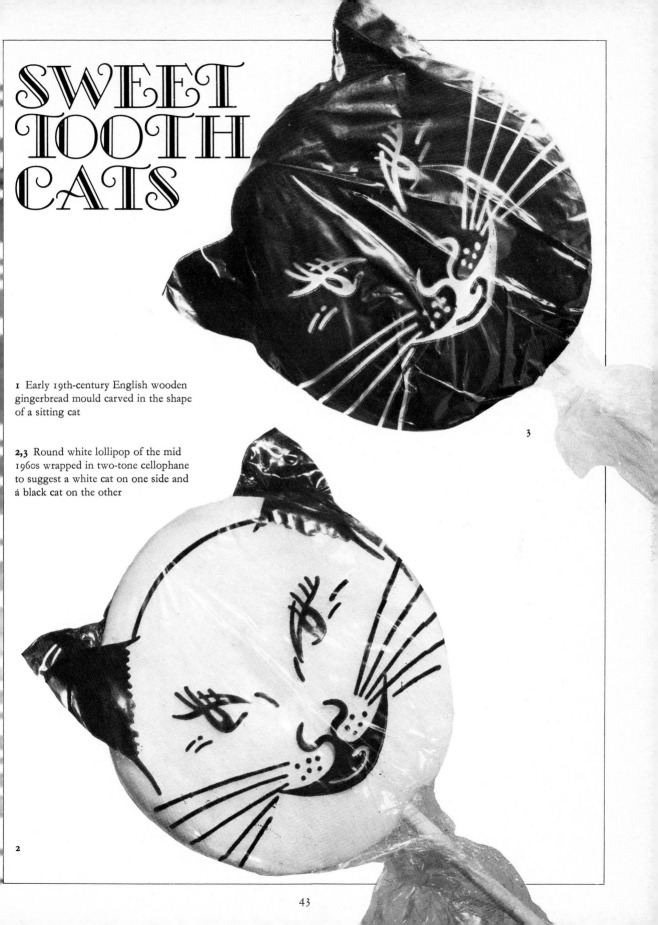

# SWEET TOOTH CATS

**1** Early 19th-century English wooden gingerbread mould carved in the shape of a sitting cat

**2,3** Round white lollipop of the mid 1960s wrapped in two-tone cellophane to suggest a white cat on one side and a black cat on the other

3

2

# Cats & Courtship

**1** *The Kittens' Wedding*, a tableau constructed in 1898 by the eccentric English taxidermist, Walter Potter (1835–1918). Taxidermy was a popular art in late 19th-century Europe when, in keeping with the mood of melancholy which emanated from the monumentally bereaved Queen Victoria, wealthy pet owners frequently had their dead cat or dog stuffed and placed under a glass dome for continuing companionship. Walter Potter went further than this usual practice by arranging his animals in human situations (a technique also employed by another taxidermist H. Ploucquet of Stuttgart) and by dressing them in appropriate clothes. Here, the kitten bride is sumptuously dressed in white brocade, with a long veil and orange blossom, and the bridesmaids wear dresses of cream or pink satin with matching blue or coral necklaces. The male wedding guests are all soberly dressed except for white buttonholes and the bride's page wears a sailor suit of blue velvet. All the guests carry tiny prayer books open at the marriage service

# A Wise Cat Answers Your Courtship Problems

QUESTION   *Dear Cat*
*Could you please tell me if there are any steps I could take to find out who will be the first in my circle of friends to marry?* CURIOUS

ANSWER   *Dear Curious*
*In America there is a folk saying that if a cat washes her face in front of several people, the first person she looks at after completing her toilet will be the first to marry. I do hope you will find this little observation useful, but please bear in mind that curiosity killed the cat.*

QUESTION   *Dear Cat*
*I am a male cat lover, but I hope you won't mind my writing to you. To put it bluntly, could you give me any guidance on the kind of woman I should choose as a wife?* PERPLEXED

ANSWER   *Dear Perplexed*
*Thank you for your letter. I am always glad to hear from male cat lovers. When choosing a wife you must follow the dictates of your own heart, but do be cautious and bear in mind the French saying that a man who loves cats will always marry an immoral woman.*

QUESTION  *Dear Cat*
*Some months ago I accidentally trod on my cat and my engagement was subsequently broken. Am I foolish in believing these two events to be in some way connected?*
CLUMSY

ANSWER  *Dear Clumsy*
*I cannot advise anyone to be too superstitious, but there is a folk belief in France that if an unmarried girl accidentally treads on a cat's tail, it will postpone her marriage day by one year. You do not say in your letter whether it was your cat's tail you trod on, but in future it might be better for your peace of mind if you imitate your poor cat and put your feet down carefully.*

QUESTION  *Dear Cat*
*Is there any advice you can give to three sisters who would like to have more suitors calling on them. Please don't tell us to get out more and join clubs.*
HUBBLE, BUBBLE AND TOIL

ANSWER  *Dear Hubble, Bubble and Toil*
*You girls should not waste any more of your money on computer dating, but would be well advised to invest it in a nice black cat instead. In England there is a sensible and well-proven folk rhyme which says:*
*Whenever the cat of the house is black,*
*The lasses of lovers will have no lack.*
*One black cat is usually more than enough for this purpose, but if you want very quick results, get three.*

**1** Mid 19th-century polychrome
chalkware cat from Pennsylvania

**2** Originally one of a pair, this mid
19th-century English earthenware tom
cat with inset glass eyes, is
distinguishable from a dog ornament by
the bow round its neck (bows were
generally reserved for cats in the 19th
century) and the desperate attempt of
the artist to give him well-defined
whiskers

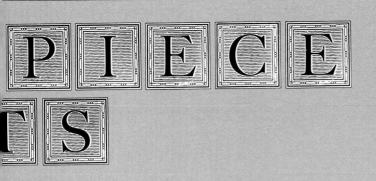

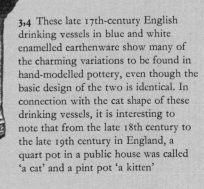

**3,4** These late 17th-century English drinking vessels in blue and white enamelled earthenware show many of the charming variations to be found in hand-modelled pottery, even though the basic design of the two is identical. In connection with the cat shape of these drinking vessels, it is interesting to note that from the late 18th century to the late 19th century in England, a quart pot in a public house was called 'a cat' and a pint pot 'a kitten'

**5** Pair of 18th-century English cats in salt-glazed ware, measuring 5 inches and 5½ inches in height respectively

**6** Late 20th-century three-piece cat ornament from Japan, consisting of a mother cat with inset green glass eyes, linked to two kittens by a chain looped through their fluffy nylon collars

**7** French white porcelain cat of the 1930s with inset blue glass eyes, one of which is now missing

**8** Late 20th-century English earthenware string dispenser modelled and painted to represent the head of a ginger cat. A ball of string fits into the cavity at the back of the mask, to be dispensed through the mouth, and a small pair of scissors is stored neatly in the loop of his blue bow

One evening and I sitting here, it was mortal cold, and the cat was curled sleeping and he on the fireflag. The wind was tearing at the thatch, and never a sound was in it if it was not the cry of the wild geese and them crossing the moon. Of a sudden he was on his feet, every hair on him standing stiff as a hackle, his back arched, his tail like a jug-handle. He stood listening. Then, with a hiss and a snarl, he was out of the door like running water. The wind died on the moment, and not one thing stirred bar the clock—the ticks of it would deafen you, like as if you had your ear to an anvil. Then the wind blew again, and a turf-sod shifted in the fire.

The next morning, with me mother and father—may God save them!— in the cart, I was driving to Mass, for it was a Sunday. We got as far as

# King Of The Cats

**1** Portrait of *Ebony* painted in watercolour on paper by Gilly Fraser *

Spooner's below, when I seen something on the road that stopped me. The whole place was one living mass of cats. In the middle was a great buck-cat, lying with his paws drawn up under him, and him looking straight in front as if there was not a living thing near him. Around him stood others and they never lifting an eye off of him. Some on the fence, and in the ditch lay more, but they were looking away from him. Here and there a small one sneaked from one lot to another, as if they were servants and they looking for orders.

'Go on,' says my father, 'or we will be late for Mass. *They are only choosing their king.*'

From George A. Little *Malachi Horan Remembers* Dublin 1943

There is no door strong enough to bar the way of the cat or a lover.

FRENCH PROVERB

I

1 Mid 19th-century French cast-iron doorstop in which the sweetly moulded face and gracefully inclined head and body line are reminiscent of illustrations by the 19th-century French artist Grandville

DOORSTOP CATS

2

**2** Painted black and white, this late 19th-century Pennsylvanian wooden doorstop in the shape of a dozing cat, has sadly lost its facial detail with the passage of time

# Smokers Cats

**1** Mid 20th-century brass clip-on case for a box of matches, decorated with a stamped pattern representing a brick wall, on top of which a painted black cat is sitting

**2** Late 19th-century bronze ash-tray in the shape of a cat's head, supported underneath by three small pointed feet

**3** Late 19th-century French ash-tray (discovered in Alexandria, Egypt) made of brass deeply embossed with a pattern representing the head of a Persian cat

**4** *The Batchelors' Party* a painting by the late 19th-century cat artist Louis Wain (1860–1939) reproduced by courtesy of Mrs B. Shoolbraid *

## The Cat And The Mouse In A Public House

A mouse pursued by a cat in a public house fell into an open barrel of whiskey. The mouse cried to the cat to be taken out of the barrel. To which the cat answered that he would only have to eat the mouse. The mouse replied:

'I don't care: anything bar to die in drink.'

The cat pawed the mouse out of the barrel, set it down, and then began to play with the mouse, which at last was able to run and escape into a hole. The cat said:

'You made a bargain that if I'd take you out of the barrel of whiskey you'd let me eat you.'

The mouse answered:

'Who gives any heed to what a fella says in drink?'

From Michael Murphey *Now You're Talking: Folk Tale From The North Of Ireland* Blackstaff Press, Belfast 1972

# CARNIVAL CATS

1

2

3

**1,2** White cat and black cat with a mouse in its mouth, two 19th-century polychrome wooden figures from an American carousel, now part of the Lady Bangor Fairground Collection at Wookey Hole, Somerset, England

**3** Late 20th-century Belgian carnival mask depicting the face of a white cat. Throughout Europe white cats are thought to be lucky, except in England, where black cats have that honour

**4** Dating from the 1930s, this black plastic cat with inset green glass eyes is one of a huge number made to this design as prizes and presents at British fairgrounds. Tiny versions of this 'lucky black cat', with painted instead of inset eyes, are still occasionally given out to passers-by by gypsies in Britain

# Diana THE RAILWAY CAT

She envies no man's hearth place—freedom's best,
  And the long run of sheds, where sacks of seed,
Oil cake, guano, Spratt's Food, and the rest,
  In hempen mountains stand,—and rat-folk breed.
These are her happy hunting grounds!—How fleet
  Amidst the bulging piles,—beneath the beams,
Hung o'er with dust-thick cobwebs,—soundless feet
  Fly scampering by; anon an engine screams.
The Railway Cat! What recks she of the noise
  Of shunting engines—shrieking steam—and loads
Of groaning, grunting wagons, men and boys:
  Is she not queen of all the Iron Roads?
She purrs, and swinging slow from paw to paw,
  Dreams,—where the charcoal brazier casts a glow,
Of moonlight raids, warm blood, and sated maw;
  Dreams that the poor tame house-cat cannot know.
Green eyes she has, like jade or chrysophrase;
  Sharp claws, and teeth to guard each kittenthing;
Ahen when the night-mail hurtles down its ways,
  She croons the lullaby all mothers sing.
And little furry faces nuzzle down;
  And tiny feeble paws claw, poke and press;
Whilst rapture of dark peace, in moon-shot gown,
  Folds round her wild maternal tenderness.
You fierce sweet daughter of a fiercer sire;
  Why should we pity? Be your comforts few,—
Yours is the crowning gift of cat's desire,—
  Freedom, above all luxury you knew.
Roaming at will amongst the silvered sacks,
  The moon-bathed silence stirred by velvet wings
Of bat-folk in the rafters,—while through cracks
  In walls and floor, a little night wind sings.
She envies no man's hearth place! Being wise,
  And craving freedom for her wild cat-soul.
What smouldering fires do gleam in those green eyes,
  What scorn of aught that savours of control!
Here reigning silent, brooding as a Sphinx
  Carven in stone, as dusk of evening spreads
Its blue-black mantle, and the first star winks
  Salaams! Diana of the Railway Sheds!

M. A. Northcote

# Holiday Cats

GOOD LUCK
FROM EASTBOURNE

GOOD LUCK
WINDSOR

ARMS OF READING

1

2

3

T A LOVELY PLACE!

SURE! IT MUST BE SOUTHEND.

*A Sermon on Sulphur*

Louis Wain.

**1** Crude earthenware souvenir figure of a lucky black cat sitting on a pouffe which bears a transfer of the municipal arms of Windsor, England

**2** This late 19th-century holiday postcard again shows a lucky black cat posing on a red plinth-like pouffe decorated with white flowers. The central portion of the postcard pulls down to release a series of photographic views of Eastbourne, England, folded in a concertina strip

**3** This tiny early 20th-century white earthenware figure of a female cat in pre-First World War sports clothes is too bizarre in its design to have originally been intended as a souvenir and it is likely that a manufacturer of souvenir ornaments bought in a batch of these figures from a more elevated source, to hastily apply transfers of the municipal arms of Reading, England. The figure is bizarre because it combines two periods of 'cat art' which are historically very widely separated: Louis Wain's late 19th-century tennis-playing cats and statues of the ancient Egyptian cat-headed goddess Bakst

**4** Striped cat sunning itself on the beach at Southend, England, an early 20th-century holiday postcard either by or in the manner of Louis Wain (1860–1939). A similar watercolour of striped cats, which is signed by Louis Wain, may be seen on page 118 and this vigorous striping is usually interpreted as marking the stage in his work before his cats are portrayed with violently jagged outlines, a characteristic of classic schizophrenic art

**5** The potted palms, fuming glasses and dubious facial expressions in this humorous postcard by Louis Wain show that these financially comfortable cats are spending part of their vacation 'taking the waters', a self-punishing exercise once pursued by the European leisured classes either at Bath or Harrogate in England, or Baden-Baden or Wildbad in Germany

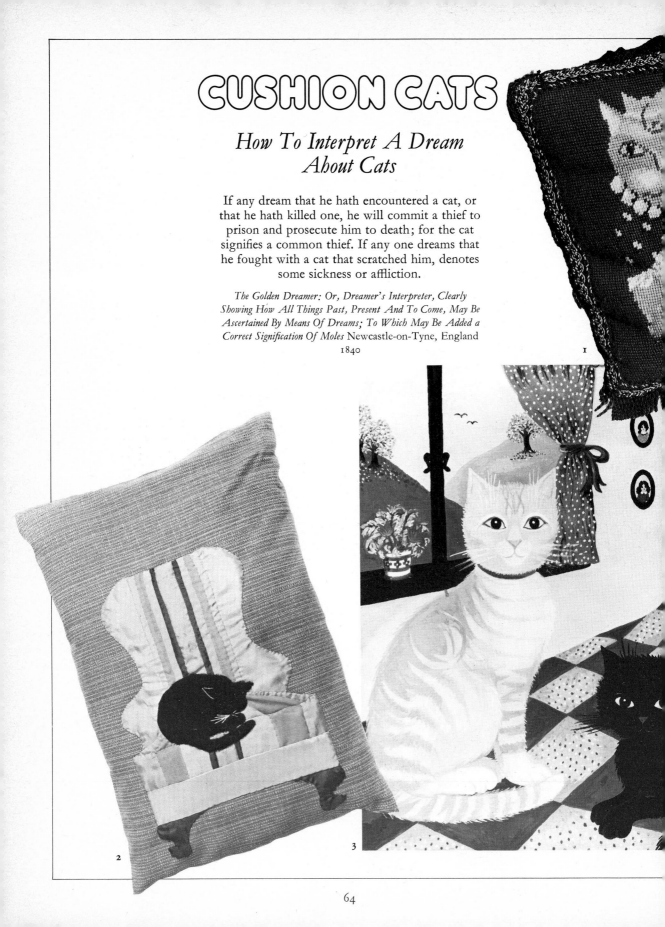

# CUSHION CATS

## How To Interpret A Dream About Cats

If any dream that he hath encountered a cat, or that he hath killed one, he will commit a thief to prison and prosecute him to death; for the cat signifies a common thief. If any one dreams that he fought with a cat that scratched him, denotes some sickness or affliction.

*The Golden Dreamer: Or, Dreamer's Interpreter, Clearly Showing How All Things Past, Present And To Come, May Be Ascertained By Means Of Dreams; To Which May Be Added a Correct Signification Of Moles* Newcastle-on-Tyne, England 1840

1 Fringed tapestry cushion entitled *Comfortable Cat,* embroidered by Nan Janvrin and reproduced by courtesy of Mrs Simon Bruton *

2 Appliqué cushion by Mrs Irena Langford depicting her cat *Pushkin* asleep on his favourite armchair. *Pushkin* is worked in black velvet and the chair in various shades of mauve satin *

3 Portrait of *Tigger* and *Footso* seated on a patchwork quilt, painted in watercolour on paper by Miss Lesley Robins *

4 Entitled *Darling Norman,* this mid 20th-century tapestry cushion depicts a black tom cat in royal robes

# 2 Three Fairytale Cats of Childhood

# The Audacious Adventures Of Puss In Boots

Although undoubtedly having its origins in the ancient oral tradition of story-telling, *Puss In Boots* first appeared in print in 1697 as *Le Maître Chat, ou le Chat Botté*, one of a collection of fairy-tales by the 17th-century French poet and critic Charles Perrault. The collection of fairy-tales appeared under the general title *Histoires et Contes du Temps Passé, avec des Moralités. Contes de ma Mère l'Oye* and was first translated into English in 1729 by Robert Samber as *Mother Goose's Tales*. Charles Perrault (1628–1703) was a warm and versatile man who, besides his strong literary interests, was also employed by Louis XIV's finance-minister Colbert as an adviser in the development of the French Academy system, which was intended to regulate education and encourage high standards of achievement in all branches of the arts, science and industry in France. Today, Perrault is best remembered for his fairy-tales and for his championing of contemporary French writers in the famous 17th-century artistic dispute between the 'Ancients' and 'Moderns'. A monument to Charles Perrault in which Puss In Boots figures magnificently may be seen in the frontispiece.

*Puss In Boots,* together with *The Sleeping Beauty* and *Cinderella,* is one of the most imaginatively potent fairy-stories in Western literature. Unlike the majority of such tales, however, it has no readily discernible moral, for the cat simply devises a series of ingenious frauds which gradually advance him and his master up the social scale until they can both retire in comfort! This lack of a moral in *Puss In Boots* worried the Victorians and at least one eminent artist was unwilling to illustrate the tale in its original form as he felt its portrayal of a charming, successful and unscrupulous adventurer who does *not* get his come-uppance was quite unsuitable for the nursery.

We, of course, feel differently. We recognise Puss In Boots as belonging to that select band of human and animal rogues who add zest to world literature and whose moral shortcomings we overlook in response to their almost tangible charm and vitality. As the illustrations in this section of the book show, it is these very qualities which have made Puss In Boots a perfect candidate for the theatre and have extended his career from the printed page to that of a pantomime star. The version of the Puss In Boots story which now follows, is taken from an edition published in Glasgow in 1845.

# A Regency Version Of Puss In Boots

### A Resolve
*Tom Malkin, a Cat,*
*Who would oft catch a rat,*
*With his species held frequent disputes;*
*To improve his exterior,*
*And make him superior,*
*Called to Hoby's, to buy him some boots.*

### Shopping
*To St James's he went,*
*And made known his intent,*
*And held up his paw for the measure;*
*A pair were soon found,*
*Which he stamped on the ground,*
*And then scampered home, with much pleasure.*

### A Beau
*To the Tailor's he frisked*
*And his merry tail whisked*
*As he gave a loud rap at the door;*
*The Tailor amazed*
*On his customer gazed,*
*And scarcely from laughter forbore.*

### Further Proofs Of Fashion
*Pantaloons, a cravat,*
*And an Opera hat,*
*Which he wore on his head à* la Russe;
*With a sword by his side,*
*Which he brandished full wide,*
*Vowing vengeance on each* plebeian *puss.*

### A Rout
*Thus equipped he went out,*
*To a Grimalkin rout,*
*Where his dress caused a number of mews,*
*But he answered their taunts,*
*By a thousand gay flaunts;*
*And talked of the fashion and news.*

### A Coquette
*Little Tib, a young puss*
*Who had oft made a fuss,*
*At the number of rats which Tom caught;*
*Was so pleased with his figure,*
*She softened her rigour,*
*And often Tom's company sought.*

### Emulation
*Says Tib, I determine*
*That velvet and ermine*
*With laces and veils, shall deck me;*
*And e'er I sleep a wink*
*Tom Malkin shall think,*
*That I, have as good taste as he.*

### A Walk
*Tibs passed by his door*
*But the rain it did pour*
*So in order to save silks and satins,*
*To get out of the slop,*
*She turned into a shop*
*And bought, a nice new pair of pattens.*

Abridged from *My Grandmother's Cat; or, Puss In Boots*
London 1811

## Overleaf

Sheet-music cover of a children's dance and lullaby from Augustus Harris's pantomime *Puss In Boots* as performed at the Theatre Royal, Drury Lane, London in December 1887. The choreographer of this particular pantomime was appropriately called Mrs Katti Lanner.

This sheet-music cover is a particularly interesting item both for collectors of theatrical ephemera and 'cat objects' as it bears in the top left-hand corner the handwritten inscription, 'With Augustus Harris's compliments.' Augustus Harris (1851–96) is generally regarded as the father of modern pantomime production in Britain and was knighted for his services to the theatre in 1891. Nicknamed 'Druriolanus' because of his connection with the Theatre Royal, Drury Lane, London, he took over the management of that theatre in the early 1880s. He transformed pantomime production by introducing lavish spectacular effects and was the first to import famous music-hall stars for such roles as the Principal Boy and the Dame, a practice still followed today with pop singers and comedians

NCE UPON A TIME there was a miller who had three sons, and when he died he divided what he possessed among them in the following manner. He gave his mill to the eldest, his ass to the second, and his cat to the youngest.

Each of the brothers accordingly took what belonged to him without the help of an attorney, who would soon have brought their little fortune to nothing in law expenses.

The poor young fellow who had nothing but the cat, complained that he was hardly used: 'My brothers,' said he, 'by joining their stocks together, may do very well in the world; but for me, when I have eaten my cat, and made a fur-cap of his skin, I may soon die of hunger!'

The cat, which all this time sat listening just inside the door of a cupboard, now ventured to come out, and addressed him as follows:

'Do not thus afflict yourself, my good master; you have only to give me a bag, and get a pair of boots made for me, so that I may scamper through the dirt and the brambles, and you shall see that you are not so ill provided for as you imagine.'

Though the cat's master did not much depend upon these promises, yet, as he had often observed the cunning tricks Puss used to catch rats and mice, such as hanging by the hind-legs, and hiding in the meal to make them believe that he was dead, he did not entirely despair of his being of some use to him in his unhappy condition.

When the cat had obtained what he asked for, he gaily began to equip himself; he drew on the boots—and, putting the bag about his neck, he took hold of the strings with his fore-paws, and, bidding his master take courage, immediately sallied forth.

The first attempt Puss made was to go into a warren, in which there was a great number of rabbits. He put some bran and some parsley into his bag; and then stretching himself out at full length, as if he was dead, he waited for some young rabbits, (which as yet knew nothing of the cunning tricks of the world,) to come and get into the bag, the better to feast upon the dainties he had put into it.

Scarcely had he lain down before he succeeded as well as could be wished. A giddy young rabbit crept into the bag and the cat immediately drew the strings and killed him without mercy.

Puss, proud of his prey, hastened directly to the palace, where he asked to speak to the king. On being shown into the apartment of his majesty, he made a low bow, and said—'I have brought you, sire, this rabbit from the warren of my lord the marquis of Carabas, who commanded me to present it to your majesty with the assurance of his respect.' This was the title the cat thought proper to bestow upon his master. 'Tell my lord marquis of Carabas,' replied the king, 'that I accept of his present with pleasure, and that I am greatly obliged to him.'

Soon after, the cat laid himself down in the same manner in a field of corn, and had as much good fortune as before; for two fine partridges got into his bag, which he immediately killed and carried to the palace; the king received them as he had done the rabbit, and ordered his servants to give the messenger something to drink. In this manner he continued to carry presents of game to the king from my lord marquis of Carabas, once at least in every week.

One day, the cat having heard that the king intended to take a ride that morning by the river-side with his daughter, who was the most beautiful princess in the world, he said to his master—'If you will but follow my advice your fortune is made. Take off your clothes, and bathe yourself in the river, just in the place I shall show you, and leave the rest to me.'

The marquis of Carabas did exactly as he was desired, without being able to guess at what the cat intended. While he was bathing the king passed by, and Puss directly called out as loud as he could bawl—'Help! help! my lord marquis of Carabas is in danger of being drowned!' The King hearing the cries, put his head out at the window of his carriage to see what was the matter; when perceiving the very cat which had brought him so many presents, he ordered his attendants to go directly to the assistance of my lord marquis of Carabas.

While they were employed in taking the marquis out of the river, the cat ran to the king's carriage, and told his majesty, that while his master was bathing, some thieves had run off with his clothes as they lay by the river-side, the cunning cat all the time having hid them under a large stone.

The king, hearing this, commanded the officers of his wardrobe to fetch one of the handsomest suits it contained, and present it to my lord marquis of Carabas, at the same time loading him with a thousand attentions. As the fine clothes they brought him made him look like a gentleman, and set off his person, which was very comely, to the greatest advantage, the king's daughter was mightily taken with his appearance, and the marquis of Carabas had no sooner cast upon her two or three respectful glances,

'When the cat had obtained what he
asked for, a pair of boots and a bag, he
gaily began to equip himself and,
bidding his master take courage,
immediately sallied forth. . . .'

## A Strange Thing That Happened To Puss's Boots

**1** In 1697 when Puss first set out on his adventures, his boots fitted him remarkably well and for two centuries they continued to fit him well . . .

**2** Suddenly, at the very end of the 19th century, some of Puss's popular illustrators seemed to forget that he needed *two* well-fitting boots to protect his feet when hunting over rough terrain, and gave him *one* very large boot instead . . .

Puss in Boots Picture Book

Illustrated by E. Caldwell

MARCUS · WARD · & · CO · L<sup>D</sup>
LONDON BELFAST & NEW YORK

3 So that by the mid 20th century, the manufacturers of everyday ornaments seemed to think that the *boot* was more important than *Puss* and left him to wonder what had gone wrong . . .

than she became violently in love with him.

The king insisted on his getting into the carriage, and taking a ride with them. The cat, enchanted to see how well his scheme was likely to succeed, ran before to a meadow that was reaping, and said to the reapers—'Good people, if you do not tell the king who will soon pass this way, that the meadow you are reaping belongs to my lord marquis of Carabas, you shall be chopped as small as minced meat.'

The king did not fail to ask the reapers to whom the meadow belonged? —'To my lord marquis of Carabas,' said they all at once; for the threats of the cat had terribly frightened them. 'You have here a very fine piece of land, my lord marquis,' said the king. 'Truly, sire,' replied he, 'it does not fail to bring me every year a plentiful harvest.'

The cat, which still went on before, now came to a field where some other labourers were making sheaves of the corn they had reaped, to whom

4 Scene from the pantomime *Puss In Boots* as performed at the Theatre Royal, Covent Garden, London in 1859

5 Scene from the pantomime *Grimalkin the Great; or, Puss In Boots and the Miller's Son* as performed at the Theatre Royal, Drury Lane, London in December 1868. Here, Puss not only wears his famous boots but a harlequin ruff as well

he said as before—'Good people, if you do not tell the king, who will presently pass this way that the corn you have reaped in this field belongs to my lord marquis of Carabas, you shall be chopped as small as minced meat.'

The king accordingly passed a moment after, and inquired to whom the corn he saw belonged?—'To my lord marquis of Carabas,' answered they very glibly; upon which the king again complimented the marquis on his noble possessions.

The cat still continued to go before, and gave the same charge to all the people he met with; so that the king was greatly astonished at the splendid fortune of my lord marquis of Carabas.

Puss at length arrived at a stately castle, which belonged to an Ogre, the richest ever known; for all the lands the king had passed through and admired were his. The cat took care to learn every particular about the Ogre, and what he could do, and then asked to speak with him, saying, as he entered the room in which he was, that he could not pass so near his castle without doing himself the honour to inquire for his health.

The Ogre received him as civilly as an Ogre could do, and desired him to be seated, 'I have been informed,' said the cat, 'that you have the gift of changing yourself into all sorts of animals; into a lion, or an elephant, for example?'—'It is very true,' replied the Ogre somewhat sternly; 'and to convince you, I will directly take the form of a lion.'—The cat was so much terrified at finding himself so near a lion, that he sprang from him, and climbed to the roof of the house; but not without much difficulty, as his boots were not very fit to walk upon the tiles.

Some minutes after, the cat perceiving that the Ogre had quitted the form of a lion, ventured to come down from the tiles, and owned that he had been a good deal frightened. 'I have been further informed,' continued the cat, 'but I know not how to believe it, that you have the power of taking the form of the smallest animals also; for example, of changing to a rat or a mouse; I confess I should think this must be impossible.'— 'Impossible! you shall see;' and at the same instant he changed himself into a mouse, and began to frisk about the room. The cat no sooner cast his eyes upon the Ogre in this form, than he sprang upon him and devoured him in an instant.

In the meantime the king, admiring, as he came near it, the magnificent castle of the Ogre, ordered his attendants to drive up to the gates, as he

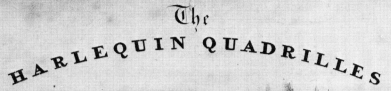

# The HARLEQUIN QUADRILLES

THE MELODIES PERFORMED AT THE

*Theatre Royal Covent Garden*

*in the Pantomime of*

## PUSS in BOOTS or the MILLERS SON

*Composed and Arranged for the*

### Piano Forte.

by

## G. F. STANSBURY.

Ent. Sta. Hall.        London, Printed & Published by Collard & Collard (late Clementi & Co.) 26, Cheapside.        Price 3'
CC

**6** Sheet-music cover of piano quadrilles arranged from melodies in the pantomime *Puss In Boots or The Miller's Son* as performed at the Theatre Royal, Covent Garden, London in 1832. The charming lithograph on this sheet-music cover contains some interesting symbolism which has very little to do with the original Puss In Boots story by Charles Perrault. The key to its strangeness is not so much the presence of a classic witch, but the fact that while protecting the cat with his left arm, the miller's son holds in his right hand a palm, symbol of victory or supreme excellence and, of course, a symbol loaded with powerful Christian connotations. It might not be too fanciful to interpret this little lithograph as heralding a turning point in the fortunes of the domestic cat. It has literally turned its back on its traditional role as the familiar of witches, Satan worshippers and eccentrics and is now historically ready for its rehabilitation as the useful but innocuous pet of that great institution, the Victorian home

7 *Thespian Puss The Panto Purr-former*, an embroidery on pink cotton by Mrs Nancy Lowther \*

wished to take a nearer view of it. The cat, hearing the noise of the carriage on the drawbridge, immediately came out, saying—'Your majesty is welcome to the castle of my lord marquis of Carabas.'—'And is this splendid castle yours also, my lord marquis of Carabas?—I never saw any thing more stately than the building, or more beautiful than the park and pleasure-grounds around it; no doubt the castle is no less magnificent within than without; pray, my lord marquis, indulge me with a sight of it.'

The marquis gave his hand to the young princess as she alighted, and followed the king, who went before. They entered a spacious hall, where they found a splendid collation which the Ogre had prepared for some friends he had that day expected to visit him; but who, hearing that the king with the princess and a great gentleman of the court were within, had not dared to enter.

The king was so much charmed with the amiable qualities and noble fortune of the marquis of Carabas, and the young princess, too, had fallen so violently in love with him, that when the king had partaken of the collation, and drank a few glasses of wine, he said to the marquis—'It will be your own fault, my lord marquis of Carabas, if you do not soon become my son-in-law.' The marquis received the intelligence with a thousand respectful acknowledgments, accepted the honour conferred upon him, and married the princess that very day.

The cat became a great lord, and never again ran after rats and mice but for his amusement.

1 Head of a white Persian cat exquisitely embroidered on an oval panel of black silk by Miss Margot Hood shortly before the First World War and reproduced here by courtesy of Mrs C. B. Stracey Clitherow *

# The White Cat

*The White Cat* is a fairy-story which has never become as widely known as *Puss In Boots,* even though it was originally published only one year after Charles Perrault presented his immortal feline hero to the world. The author of *The White Cat,* or *La Chatte Blanche* as it was originally known, was a French novelist and memoirist, Marie-Catherine Jumel de Barneville, Comtesse d'Aulnoy (*circa* 1650–1705) whose output of fairy-stories for children has now largely fallen into obscurity with the exception of *The White Cat* and *The Yellow Dwarf* which both appeared in a collection entitled simply *Contes des Fées* in 1698. It is no coincidence that the Comtesse d'Aulnoy and Charles Perrault were both French and both writing fairy-stories during the same period, for these enchanting tales are but one example of the delicate and frivolously imaginative art which the French aristocracy developed and enjoyed in the centuries immediately preceding the French Revolution. The development of ballet at the 17th-century French court is another example of this refined and wayward spirit and as the caption on page 90 demonstrates, these two art forms are closely linked.

Although the Comtesse d'Aulnoy did not write her fairy-stories with the disarming simplicity of Perrault and preferred to make them longer and more complicated in plotting—factors which perhaps combine to make them lose something in immediacy —there is much in *The White Cat* to be enjoyed. Foremost in this enjoyment is the Comtesse d'Aulnoy's portrayal of the charming love affair between her heroine and the young prince, which ultimately leads him to exclaim, 'Alas! How it will afflict me to leave you whom I love so much! Either make yourself a lady or make me a cat!' Together with opulent and exotic descriptions of the White Cat's enchanted palace in the depths of a forest, this fairy-story conveys the mood of mystery and sensuous strangeness which cat lovers have always associated with their own pets.

Then there is the personality of the White Cat herself, beautiful, self-possessed, intelligent, perfect in courtesy and always conveying an air of delicate melancholy. 'Aristocatic' both in manner and, of course, dress, there is a great similarity between the Comtesse d'Aulnoy's descriptions of her heroine and the fashionable female cats drawn by another French artist, the great illustrator Jean Ignace Isidore Gérard (1803–47), some of whose works are shown on pages 47 and 92.

Perhaps better known under his professional pseudonym, 'Grandville', this artist had a satirical genius for illustrating birds and animals of every kind in the clothes and surroundings of well-defined human types. Thus, in his most famous collection of illustrations, *Scènes de la Vie Privée et Publique des Animaux* published in Paris in 1842 (and containing short texts by Honoré de Balzac and George Sand among many others) Grandville chose the white short-hair cat as the perfect animal counterpart to the mid 19th-century Parisian lady of fashion, with her taste for wantonly luxurious dress and amorous intrigues. It was part of Grandville's genius that the clothes he gave his white cats—the bonnets, muffs, ball-dresses and lawn shifts—blend perfectly with the animals' personalities and do not foolishly insult them (lovers of poodle wellingtons please note). In Grandville's work this blend of the human type satirized and the animal chosen to convey the satire is so perfectly achieved, that I for one find it difficult to look at a white cat without seeing it through Grandville's eyes as a mid 19th-century fashion plate. As an imaginative Frenchman with an obvious love and understanding of animals, Grandville must have known the Comtesse d'Aulnoy's fairy-story and found in it the inspiration for his own portrayal of white cats.

But the White Cat does not live in the printed page alone. Like her colleagues Puss In Boots and Dick Whittington's companion, Mouser, she is also a theatrical performer, in this case not in pantomime but in the 19th-century Russian ballet. On stage, the White Cat made her *début* at the Maryinsky Theatre, St Petersburg on 15th January 1890 as a wedding guest in the ballet *The Sleeping Beauty* for which music was composed by Peter Ilyitch Tchaikowsky and choreography by Marius Petipa. An illustration and further information about the White Cat's appearance in this ballet may be found on page 90. The version of the fairy-story *The White Cat* which now follows, has been abridged from an edition published in Edinburgh and London in 1847.

NCE UPON A TIME, a King had three sons, all remarkably handsome in their persons, and in their tempers generous and noble. Some wicked courtiers made the King believe that the Princes were impatient to wear his crown, and that they were contriving a plot to deprive him of his sceptre and authority.

The King felt that he was growing old, but as he found himself as capable of governing as ever, he had no inclination to resign his power; and, therefore, that he might pass the rest of his days peaceably, he determined to employ the Princes in such a manner, as at once to give each of them the hope of succeeding to the Crown, and fill up the time they might otherwise have spent in so undutiful a manner.

He sent for them to his cabinet, and after conversing with them kindly, he added: 'You must be sensible, my dear children, that my great age prevents me from attending so closely as I have hitherto done to state affairs. I fear this may be injurious to my subjects; I therefore desire to place my crown on the head of one of you; but it is no more than just, that in return for such a present, you should procure me some amusement in my retirement, for I shall leave the capital for ever. I cannot help thinking, that a little dog, that should be handsome, faithful, and engaging, would be the very thing to make me happy; so that, without bestowing a preference on any one of you, I declare, that he who brings me the most perfect little dog shall be my successor. The Princes were much surprised at the fancy of their father to have a little dog; yet they accepted the proposition with pleasure: and accordingly, after taking leave of the King, who presented them with abundance of money and jewels, and appointed that day twelvemonth for their return, they set off on their travels.

Each took a different road; but we intend to relate the adventures of only the youngest, who was the handsomest, most amiable, and accomplished prince that could be imagined.

At length, wandering he knew not whither, he found himself in a forest; night suddenly came on, and with it a violent storm of thunder, lightning, and rain: to add to his perplexity, he lost his path, and could find no way out of the forest. When he had groped about for a long time, he perceived a light, which made him suppose he was not far from some house: he accordingly pursued his way toward it, and in a short time found himself at the gates of the most magnificent palace ever beheld. The door that

I LOVE A CUDDLE.

1 *I Love A Cuddle*, a late 19th-century hand-tinted novelty postcard

**2 Previous page** *When Tommy Comes Marching Home*, a late 19th-century popular print reproduced by courtesy of Mrs H. M. Bate*

**3 Left** *Two Cats In A Basket*, an oil painting in *pointilliste* technique by the leading British naive painter James Lloyd (1905–74)

**4 Above** Portrait miniature of *Supreme*, a fine ginger cat, painted in watercolour on vellum by Aubrey Claringbold*

**5 Overleaf left** Portrait of *Snoo* painted in oil on board by Mrs E. Akid in 1969*

**6 Overleaf right** *Curiosity Cat*, painted in oil on paper-backed canvas by Paul J. Tuttle in 1976*

P.J.Tuttle. 1976.

W. SCHWAR.

**7 Previous page** *A Friend Of The Family*, a sentimental picture painted in Austria in the late 19th century

**8 Left** Tapestry portrait by Alexandra Artley of her own cat, *Flora*

**9 Above** Portrait of her cat *Buster* in a favourite sleeping position painted in watercolour on paper by Mrs B. G. Ludgate*

**10 Overleaf** *Meet My Dancing Partner*, one of a series of ballroom postcards by the late 19th-century popular cat artist, Louis Wain

Bedroom Cat : Helen Williams 7·76

11 **Left** Made of paper, this children's party novelty of the 1920s contains a central concertina strip which produces a 'jumping' movement in the cat

12 **Above** *Bedroom Cat*, a silver-framed miniature, measuring 1¾ × 2¼ inches, painted in oil on wood by Helen Williams in 1976 and reproduced by courtesy of the Portal Gallery, London

**13** *Great British Cat*, painted in oil
on board by Andrew Murray and
reproduced by courtesy of the Portal
Gallery, London

2 Frontispiece to an English-language
edition of *The White Cat* published in
Edinburgh and London in 1847. Here,
the illustrator has interpreted the
Comtesse d'Aulnoy's exotic descriptions
of the White Cat's enchanted palace in
terms of ancient Egyptian architecture
and has portrayed the feline heroine of
the fairy-story as a languishing
Cleopatra-like princess

opened into it was made of gold, covered with sapphire stones, which cast so resplendent a brightness over every thing around, that scarcely could the strongest eye-sight bear to look at it: this was the light the Prince had seen from the forest. The walls of the building were of transparent porcelain, variously coloured, representing the history of all the fairies that had existed from the beginning of the world.

In a few moments the door was opened; but he perceived nothing but twelve hands in the air, each holding a torch. The Prince was so astonished that he durst not move a step; when he felt himself pushed gently on by some other hands from behind him. He walked on in great perplexity; and to be secure from danger, he put his hand upon his sword: he entered a vestibule inlaid with porphyry and lapis-lazuli, when the most melodious voice he had ever heard chanted the following words:

'Welcome, prince, no danger fear,
Mirth and love attend you here;
You shall break the magic spell,
That on a beauteous maiden fell;
Welcome, prince, no danger fear,
Mirth and love attend you here!'

The Prince now advanced with confidence, wondering what these words could mean; the hands moved him forward toward a large door of coral, which opened of itself to give him admittance into a splendid apartment built of mother-of-pearl, through which he passed into others so richly adorned with paintings and jewels, and so resplendently lighted with thousands of lamps, girandoles, and lustres, that the Prince imagined he must be in an enchanted palace.

As he was reflecting on the wonderful things he had seen in this palace, his attention was suddenly caught by a small figure, which just then entered the room, and advanced towards him. It wore a long black veil, and was supported by two cats in mourning, and with swords by their sides; they were followed by a numerous retinue of cats, some carrying cages full of rats, and others mouse-traps full of mice.

The Prince was at a loss what to think. The little figure now approached, and throwing aside her veil, he beheld a most beautiful white cat: she seemed young and melancholy, and addressing herself to the Prince, she said, 'Young Prince, you are welcome; your presence affords me the greatest pleasure.'—'Madam,' replied the Prince, 'I would fain thank you for your generosity, nor can I help observing that you must be a most extraordinary creature, to possess, with your present form, the gift of speech, and the magnificent palace I have seen.'—'All this is very true,' answered the beautiful cat; 'but, Prince, I am not fond of talking, and least of all do I like compliments; let us therefore sit down to supper.'

The trunkless hands then placed the dishes on the table, and the Prince and the white cat seated themselves. The first dish was made of young pigeons, and the next was a fricassee of the fattest mice imaginable: the view of the other made the Prince almost afraid to taste the other, till the white cat, who guessed his thoughts, assured him that there were certain dishes at table in which there was not a single morsel of either rat or mouse, and that these had been dressed expressly for him: accordingly he ate heartily of such as she recommended.

When supper was over, the Prince perceived that the white cat had a portrait set in gold hanging to one of her feet. He begged her permission to look at it; when what was his astonishment to see the portrait of a handsome young man, exactly resembling himself! He said to himself, there was something very extraordinary in all this; yet as the white cat sighed, and looked very sorrowful, he did not venture to ask any questions.

**4** A glimpse of the *pas de deux* for the
White Cat and Puss In Boots from Act
III of the ballet *The Sleeping Beauty*, first
performed at St Petersburg in 1890.
Based on Charles Perrault's fairy-tale
*La Belle au Bois Dormant*, this ballet tells
the familiar story of Princess Aurora
who, cursed at her christening by a
wicked fairy, pricks her finger on a
spindle and is condemned to sleep for a
hundred years until awakened by a kiss
from Prince Charming.

In Act III of the ballet Princess Aurora
and Prince Charming are married and a
succession of fairy-tale characters arrive
as wedding guests to entertain the
assembled courtiers with their dances.
The first to arrive are the Gold, Silver,
Sapphire and Diamond Fairies. Then
come the White Cat and Puss In Boots
who dance a portrayal of feline love as
the oboes in Tchaikowsky's score
imitate cats' voices. At first they are full
of affection. Then, tiring of his
attentions, the White Cat scratches Puss
In Boots and runs off. He leaps after
her and apparently the two cats are
reconciled behind the scenes, because
they return to join all the other guests
and courtiers in the joyful mazurka
which closes the ballet!

90

He conversed with her on different subjects, and found her extremely well versed in every thing that was passing in the world.

When night was far advanced, the white cat wished him a good night, and he was conducted by the hands to his bed-chamber, which was different still from any thing he had seen in the palace, being hung with the wings of butterflies, mixed with the most curious feathers. His bed was of gauze, festooned with bunches of the gayest ribbands, and the looking-glasses reached from the floor to the ceiling.

After that every day was spent in new amusements; and this life of pleasure made him forget that he was to procure a little dog for the old king. He thought no longer of any thing but of pleasing the sweet little creature who received him so courteously.

The Prince had almost forgot his country and relations, and sometimes even regretted that he was not a cat, so great was his affection for his mewing companions. 'Alas!' said he to the white cat, 'how will it afflict me to leave you whom I love so much! Either make yourself a lady, or make me a cat!' She smiled at the Prince's wish; but made him scarcely any reply.

At length the twelvemonth was nearly expired: the white cat, who knew the very day when the Prince was to reach his father's palace, reminded him that he had but three days longer to look for a perfect little dog. The Prince, astonished at his own forgetfulness, began to afflict himself; when the cat told him not to be sorrowful, since she would not only provide him with a little dog, but also with a horse which should convey him safely in less than twelve hours. 'Look here,' said she, showing him an acorn, 'this contains what you desire.' The Prince put the acorn to his ear, and heard the barking of a little dog. Transported with joy, he thanked the cat a thousand times, and the next day bidding her tenderly adieu, he set out on his return.

Next day at the palace the king examined the two little dogs of the elder princes, and declared he thought them so equally beautiful, that he knew not to which, with justice, he could give the preference. They accordingly began to dispute, when the youngest prince, taking the acorn from his pocket, soon ended their contention; for a little dog appeared which could with ease go through the smallest ring, and was besides a miracle of beauty.

The king could not possibly hesitate in declaring his satisfaction; yet as

5 White cat dressed in the winter street clothes of a mid 19th-century Parisian lady of fashion from *Scènes de la Vie Privée et Publique des Animaux,* published in 1842 with illustrations by Jean Isidore Gérard. Working under the professional peudonym, 'Grandville', this great French animal illustrator was born at Nancy in 1803 and after first studying miniature painting, he devoted himself to the newly-discovered invention of lithography. After a prolific working life as a satirical animal illustrator for a wide variety of periodicals and books, he died in a lunatic asylum at Vanves, near Paris, in 1847. Another example of this artist's work may be seen on page 47

he was not more inclined than the year before to part with his crown, he could think of nothing more to his purpose than telling his sons that he was extremely obliged to them for the pains they had taken; and that, since they had succeeded so well, he could not but wish they would make a second attempt: he therefore begged they would take another year for procuring him a piece of cambric, so fine as to be drawn through the eye of a small needle.

The three princes thought this very hard; yet they set out in obedience to the king's command. The two eldest took different roads, and the youngest remounted his horse, and in a short time arrived at the palace of his beloved white cat, who received him with the greatest joy, while the trunkless hands helped him, as before, to dismount, and provided him with immediate refreshment; after which the Prince gave the white cat an account of the admiration which had been bestowed on the beautiful little dog, and informed her of his father's further injunction.

'Make yourself perfectly easy, dear Prince,' said she; 'I have in my palace some cats that are particularly expert in making such cambric as the king requires; so you have nothing to do but to give me the pleasure of your company while it is making; and I will take care to procure you all the amusement possible.' She accordingly ordered the most curious fireworks to be immediately played off in sight of the window of the apartment in which they were sitting; and nothing but festivity and rejoicing was heard throughout the palace for the Prince's return.

As the white cat continually gave proofs of an excellent understanding, the Prince was by no means tired of her company. She talked with him of state affairs, of theatres, of fashions; in short, she was at a loss on no subject whatever; so that when the Prince was alone he had plenty of amusement in thinking how it could possibly be that a small white cat could be endowed with all the powers of human creatures.

The twelvemonth in this manner again passed insensibly away; but the cat took care to remind the Prince of his duty in proper time. 'For once, my Prince,' said she, 'I will have the pleasure of equipping you as suits your high rank;' when, looking into the court-yard, he saw a superb car, ornamented all over with gold, silver, pearl, and diamonds, drawn by twelve horses as white as snow, and harnessed in the most sumptuous trappings; and behind the car a thousand guards, richly apparelled, were in waiting to attend the Prince's person.

She then presented him with a nut: 'You will find in it,' said she, 'the piece of cambric I promised you; do not break the shell till you are in the presence of the king your father.' Then, to prevent the acknowledgements he was about to offer, she hastily bade him adieu.

Nothing could exceed the speed with which the snow-white horses conveyed this fortunate prince to his father's palace, where his brothers had just arrived before him. When it was the youngest prince's turn to present his piece of cambric, he opened a magnificent little box, inlaid with jewels, took out a walnut and cracked the shell, imagining he should immediately perceive his piece of cambric; but what was his astonishment to see nothing but a filbert! He did not, however, lose his hopes; he cracked the filbert, and it presented him with a cherry-stone. The cherry-stone was filled with a kernel; he divided it, and found in the middle a grain of wheat, and in that a grain of millet-seed. He was now absolutely confounded, and could not help muttering between his teeth, 'Oh, white cat! white cat! thou hast deceived me!' At this instant he felt his hand severely scratched by the claw of a cat: upon which he again took courage, and, opening the grain of millet-seed, to the astonishment of all present, he drew from it a piece of cambric four hundred yards in length, and fine enough to be drawn, with perfect ease, through the eye of the needle.

When the king found he had no pretext left for refusing the crown to his youngest son, he sighed deeply, and it was plain to be seen that he was sorry for the Prince's success. 'My sons,' said he, 'it is so gratifying to the heart of a father to receive proofs of his children's love and obedience, that I cannot refuse myself the satisfaction of requiring of you one thing more. You must undertake another expedition; and whichever of you, by the end of a year, shall bring me the most beautiful lady, shall marry her, and obtain my crown.'

So the princes again took leave of the king, and of each other, and set out without delay, and in less than twelve hours our young Prince again arrived in his splendid car at the palace of his dear white cat, who received him as before. He gave her an account of all that had passed, and the new request of the king his father. 'Never mind it, my Prince,' said, she 'I engage to provide you with what you want; and, in the meantime, let us be as merry as we can; for it is only when I have the pleasure of your company that I am the least inclined to entertainments or rejoicings of any kind.'

At length only one day remained of the year, when the white cat thus addressed him:—'Tomorrow, my Prince, you must present yourself at the palace of your father, and give him a proof of your obedience. It depends only on yourself to conduct thither the most beautiful princess ever yet beheld: for the time is come when the enchantment by which I am bound may be ended. *You must cut off my head and tail,*' continued she, '*and throw them into the fire.*'—'I!' answered the Prince hastily, 'I cut off your head and tail! You surely mean to try my affection, which, believe me, beautiful cat, is truly yours.'—'You mistake me, generous prince,' said she, 'I do not doubt your regard; but if you wish to see me in any other form but that of a cat, you must consent to do as I desire: when you

Portrait of *La Duchessa*, painted in
atercolour on paper by Miss
. I. Covell, showing a female cat in
uritanian court dress *

will have done me a service I shall never be able sufficiently to repay you.'

The Prince's eyes filled with tears as he spoke, yet he considered himself obliged to undertake the dreadful task; and the cat continuing to press him with the greatest eagerness, with a trembling hand he drew his sword, cut off her head and tail, and threw them into the fire. No sooner was this done, than the most beautiful lady his eyes had ever seen stood before him; and her train of attendants, who at the same moment as their mistress were changed to their natural shapes, came to offer their congratulations to the queen, and inquire her commands. She received them with great kindness; and then ordering them to withdraw, she thus addressed the astonished Prince:

'Do not imagine, dear Prince, that I have been always a cat, or that I am of obscure birth. My father was the monarch of six kingdoms. Circumstances, which it would take too long now to narrate, drew on him and my mother the malice of a cruel fairy. She revenged herself on them through me, their only child, by changing me into a cat, along with all my servants. She then placed me in this palace, gave me the hands you have seen as attendants, attached this portrait to my wrist, and decreed that I should not be restored to my natural figure, till a young prince, of whom it was the perfect resemblance, should cut off and burn my head and tail. You, my Prince, are that perfect resemblance; and, accordingly, you have ended the enchantment. I need not add, that I already love you more than my life; let us, therefore, hasten to the palace of the king your father, and obtain his approbation to our marriage.'

The Prince and Princess accordingly set out side by side in a car of still greater splendour than before, and reached the palace just as the two brothers had arrived with two beautiful princesses.

The king, hearing that each of his sons had succeeded in finding what he had required, again began to think of some new expedient to delay the time of resigning his crown; but when the whole court were with the king assembled to pass judgment, the princess who accompanied the youngest, perceiving his thoughts by his countenance, stepped majestically forward, and thus addressed him:

'What pity that your Majesty, who is so capable of governing, should think of resigning the crown! I am fortunate enough to have six kingdoms in my possession; permit me to bestow one on each of the elder princes, and to enjoy the remaining four in the society of the youngest. And may it please your Majesty to keep your own kingdom, and to make no decision concerning the beauty of the three princesses, who, without such a proof of your Majesty's preference, will no doubt live happily together!'

The air resounded with the applauses of the assembly: the young prince and princess embraced the king, and next their brothers and sisters: the three weddings immediately took place, and the kingdoms were divided as the princess had proposed, in each of which nothing for a long time prevailed but rejoicings.

# The History Of Dick Whittington And His Cat

Unlike *Puss In Boots* and *The White Cat,* the story of Dick Whittington and his cat is not a formally composed fairy-tale, but the imperfectly remembered biography of a real citizen in medieval London, to which pleasing additions have been made throughout the centuries. Richard Whittington (*circa* 1358–1423) was the third son of Sir William Whittington of Pauntley, Gloucestershire, England and was apprenticed in approximately 1371 to a member of the Mercers' Company in London, generally thought to be Sir John Fitzwarren whose daughter, Alice, Whittington subsequently married. Legend has been helped by the curious fact that when he was only 21 and his apprenticeship just over, Whittington was sufficiently wealthy to make a modest contribution to a city loan, and increasing both in wealth and prestige, he became Lord Mayor of London in 1397, 1398, 1406 and for the last time in 1419.

At the height of his career Richard Whittington commanded such huge financial resources that he regularly loaned money to the English Crown, but he is best remembered in the City of London for the genuinely charitable purposes to which he directed part of his wealth, writing of this in his will:

'The fervent desire and busy intention of a prudent, wise and devout man should be to cast before and make secure the state and end of this short life with deeds of mercy and pity. Especially to provide for those miserable persons whom age, penury or poverty insulteth and to whom the power of seeking the necessaries of life by act and bodily labour is interdicted.'

The Jacobean actor-dramatists Thomas Heywood and William Rowley listed Whittington's acts of charity in their play *Fortune By Land And Sea* in 1609 and they include, both before and after his death, the erection of thirteen almshouses for poor men, the paving and glazing of the Guildhall, London, the gift of a library to Greyfriars Priory, the gift of another library to the Guildhall which was later dispersed by the Duke of Somerset during the

1 Mouser protecting her master, Dick Whittington, from a gang of marauding elves on Highgate Hill, London: a scene from Augustus Harris's pantomime *Whittington And His Cat* as performed

at the Theatre Royal, Drury Lane, London in 1884. A biographical note about Augustus Harris, the father of modern pantomime production in Britain may be found on page 69

English Reformation, the repairing of St Bartholomew's church, Smithfield, the rebuilding of Newgate Prison and the establishment of a free public water supply for the poor. Despite these considerable acts of beneficence and his financial services to the English Crown, there is no record that Whittington ever was knighted. He was buried in the church of St Michael, Paternoster Royal, in which his grave was subsequently disturbed three times before both tomb and church were swept away in the Great Fire of London in 1666.

These are the basic facts of the real Richard Whittington's life and the classic biography to which serious accounts of his life are still indebted is the Reverend Samuel Lyon's book *The Model Merchant Of The Middle Ages* published in 1860. The two disputed areas of Whittington's life on which 'fairy-tale' and pantomime versions have elaborated is whether or not he really was a penniless boy when first seeking his fortune in London and secondly, what part his famous cat had in his rapid ascent, if indeed, it existed at all.

As Whittington's father was a knight it is generally thought that he did in fact have a better start in life than the majority of his contemporaries and the romantic 'rags to riches' element in the pantomime version of his life is thought to have come from a lost play of 1605 called *The History of Richard Whittington, of his Lowe Byrth, His Great Fortune, as it was Plaied by the Prynces Servants*. The cat, however, in true feline fashion, has not lent itself to any definite scholarly conclusions. As Whittington is said to have had his first financial success by exporting his cat by ship to an eastern country then plagued by mice and rats, the assault on the 'cat problem' is nowadays usually etymological as traditional naval language is awash with slang terms all beginning with the word 'cat'. On the other hand, the Reverend Samuel Lyons, Whittington's most accredited biographer, was prepared to find in favour of a real cat on the basis of archaelogical evidence. A 15th-century figure of a boy with a cat was found at a house in Gloucester which the Whittington family had occupied until 1460 and the historian William Maitland (1693–1757) noted in his *History of London from its Foundation by the Romans to the Present Time* . . . , published in 1739, that when Newgate Prison was rebuilt after the Great Fire there was found a figure of a boy with the word 'Libertas' carved on the hat and a cat at its feet. A similar statue is alluded to at the end of the Dick Whittington story which now follows, abridged from an edition published in Glasgow in 1845.

NCE UPON A TIME in the reign of the famous King Edward the Third, there was a little boy called Dick Whittington, whose father and mother died when he was very young, so that he remembered nothing at all about them, and was left a dirty little fellow running about a country village. As poor Dick was not old enough to work, he was in a sorry plight; he got but little for his dinner, and sometimes nothing at all for his breakfast; for the people who lived in the village were very poor themselves, and could spare him little more than the parings of potatoes, and now and then a hard crust.

One day a waggoner, with a large waggon and eight horses, all with bells at their heads, drove through the village while Dick was lounging near his favourite sign-post. The thought immediately struck him that it must be going to the fine town of London; and taking courage he asked the waggoner to let him walk with him by the side of the waggon. The man, hearing from poor Dick that he had no parents, and seeing by his ragged condition that he could not be worse off, told him he might go if he would: so they set off together.

Dick got safe to London: and so eager was he to see the fine streets paved all over with gold, that he ran as fast as his legs would carry him through several streets, expecting every moment to come to those that were all paved with gold; for Dick had three times seen a guinea in his own village, and observed what a great deal of money it brought in change; so he imagined he had only to take up some little bits of the pavement, to have as much money as he desired.

Poor Dick ran till he was tired, and at last, finding it grow dark, and that whichever way he turned he saw nothing but dirt instead of gold, he sat down in a dark corner, and cried himself asleep.

Little Dick remained all night in the 'streets; and next morning, finding himself very hungry, he got up and walked about, asking those he met to give him a halfpenny to keep him from starving; but nobody staid to answer him, and only two or three gave him any thing; so that the poor boy was soon in the most miserable condition. Being almost starved to death, he laid himself down at the door of one Mr. Fitzwarren, a great rich merchant. Here he was soon perceived by the cook-maid, who was an ill-tempered creature, and happened just then to be very busy dressing dinner for her master and mistress: so, seeing poor Dick, she called out,

2 Miss Queenie Leighton as Dick and Mr G. Ali as Mouser, appropriately framed by cats' heads, in a scene from the pantomime *Dick Whittington* as performed at the Theatre Royal, Drury Lane, London in December 1908. In comparison with the beautifully made cat costume shown in this photograph by Bassano, the standard of cat costume design in today's pantomime productions is enough to make a cat laugh

**3** Looking back over her shoulder towards the City of London, this elegant statue of Dick Whittington's cat was erected on Highgate Hill, London in 1821, thirteen years after the almshouses which Whittington had originally built for poor men on the north side of St Michael's, Paternoster Royal were removed from the City of London to Highgate. The fact that the cat is glancing backwards is an allusion to that part of the Whittington legend in which young Dick, at first defeated by poverty and abuse in London, was climbing Highgate Hill to return to the provinces when the Bow-bells of London rang out their prophecy: 'Turn again, Whittington, Lord Mayor of London.'

'What business have you there, you lazy rogue? There is nothing else but beggars; if you do not take yourself away, we will see how you will like a sousing of some dish-water I have here that is hot enough to make you caper?'

Just at this time Mr. Fitzwarren himself came home from the city to dinner, and seeing a dirty ragged boy lying at the door, said to him, 'Why do you lie there, my lad? You seem old enough to work. I fear you must be somewhat idle.'—'No, indeed, Sir,' says Whittington, 'that is not true, for I would work with all my heart, but I know nobody, and I believe I am very sick for want of food.'—'Poor fellow!' answered Mr. Fitzwarren.

Dick now tried to rise, but was obliged to lie down again, being too weak to stand; for he had not eaten any thing for three days, and was no longer able to run about and beg a halfpenny of people in the streets: so the kind merchant ordered that he should be taken into his house, and have a good dinner immediately, and that he should be kept to do what dirty work he was able for the cook.

Little Dick would have lived very happily in this worthy family, had it not been for the crabbed cook, who was finding fault and scolding at him from morning till night; and was withal so fond of roasting and basting, that, when the spit was out of her hands, she would be at basting poor Dick's head and shoulders with a broom, or any thing else that happened to fall in her way; till at last her ill usage of him was told to Miss Alice, Mr. Fitzwarren's daughter, who asked the ill-tempered creature if she was not ashamed to use a little friendless boy so cruelly; and added, she would certainly be turned away if she did not treat him with more kindness.

But though the cook was so ill-tempered, Mr. Fitzwarren's footman was quite the contrary: he had lived in the family many years, was rather elderly, and had once a little boy of his own, who died when about the age of Whittington; so he could not but feel compassion for the poor boy.

As the footman was very fond of reading, he used generally in the evening to entertain his fellow-servants, when they had done their work, with some amusing book. The pleasure our little hero took in hearing him made him very much desire to learn to read too; so the next time the good-natured footman gave him a halfpenny, he bought a horn-book with it; and, with a little of his help, Dick soon learned his letters, and afterwards to read.

Besides the ill-humour of the cook, which now, however, was somewhat mended, Whittington had another hardship to get over. This was, that his bed, which was of flock, was placed in a garret, where there were so many holes in the floor and walls, that he never went to bed without being awakened in his sleep by great numbers of rats and mice, which generally ran over his face, and made such a noise, that he sometimes thought the walls were tumbling down about him.

One day a gentleman who paid a visit to Mr. Fitzwarren, happened to have dirtied his shoes, and begged they might be cleaned. Dick took great pains to make them shine, and the gentleman gave him a penny. This he resolved to lay out in buying a cat, if possible; and the next day, seeing a little girl with a cat under her arm, he went up to her, and asked if she would let him have it for a penny; to which the girl replied, she would with all her heart, for her mother had more cats than she could maintain; adding, that the one she had was an excellent mouser.

This cat Whittington hid in the garret, always taking care to carry her a part of his dinner: and in a short time he had no further disturbance from the rats and mice, but slept as sound as a top.

Soon after this, the merchant, who had a ship ready to sail, richly laden, and thinking it but just that all his servants should have some chance for good luck as well as himself, called them into the parlour, and asked them what commodity they chose to send.

All mentioned something they were willing to venture but poor Whittington, who, having no money nor goods, could send nothing at all, for which reason he did not come in with the rest; but Miss Alice, guessing what was the matter, ordered him to be called, and offered to lay down some money for him from her own purse; but this, the merchant observed, would not do, for it must be something of his own.

Upon this, poor Dick said, he had nothing but a cat, which he bought for a penny that was given him.

'Fetch thy cat, boy,' says Mr. Fitzwarren, 'and let her go.'

Whittington brought poor puss, and delivered her to the captain with tears in his eyes; for he said, 'He should now again be kept awake all night by the rats and mice.'

All the company laughed at the oddity of Whittington's adventure; and Miss Alice, who felt the greatest pity for the poor boy, gave him some halfpence to buy another cat.

This and several other marks of kindness shown him by Miss Alice,

4 Woodcut from a late 18th-century ballad-sheet showing Whittington and his cat awaiting the approach of *The Unicorn*, the ship on which Whittington traditionally 'exported' his cat to an eastern country plagued with rats and mice. The right-hand panel of the woodcut shows three bell-ringers and is an allusion to the peal of Bow-bells which caused Whittington to 'turn again' on Highgate Hill, London

made the ill-tempered cook so jealous of the favours the poor boy received, that she began to use him more cruelly than ever, and constantly made game of him for sending his cat to sea; asking him, if he thought it would sell for as much money as would buy a halter.

At last, the unhappy little fellow, being unable to bear this treatment any longer, determined to run away from his place: he accordingly packed up the few things that belonged to him, and set out very early in the morning on Allhallow Day, which is the first of November. He travelled as far as Holloway, and there sat down on a stone, which to this day is called Whittington's Stone, and began to consider what course he should take.

While he was thus thinking what he could do, Bow-bells, of which there were then only six, began to ring; and it seemed to him that their sounds addressed him in this manner:

'Turn again, Whittington,
Lord Mayor of London.'

'Lord Mayor of London!' says he to himself. 'Why, to be sure, I would bear any thing to be Lord Mayor of London, and ride in a fine coach! Well, I will go back, and think nothing of all the cuffing and scolding of old Cicely, if I am at last to be Lord Mayor of London.'

So back went Dick, and got into the house, and set about his business, before Cicely came down stairs.

The ship, with the cat on board, was long beaten about at sea, and was at last driven by contrary winds on a part of the coast of Barbary, inhabited by Moors that were unknown to the English.

The natives in this country came in great numbers, out of curiosity, to see the people on board, who were all of so different a colour from themselves, and treated them with great civility, and, as they became better acquainted, showed marks of eagerness to purchase the fine things with which the ship was laden.

The captain, seeing this, sent patterns of the choicest articles he had to the king of the country, who was so much pleased with them, that he sent for the captain and his chief mate to the palace. Here they were placed, as is the custom of the country, on rich carpets flowered with gold and silver: and the king and queen being seated at the upper end of the room, dinner was brought in, which consisted of the greatest rarities. No sooner, however, were the dishes set before the company, than an amazing number of rats and mice rushed in, and helped themselves plentifully from every dish, scattering pieces of flesh and gravy all about the room.

The captain, extremely astonished, asked if these vermin were not very offensive?

'Oh, yes,' said they, 'very offensive; and the king would give half his treasure to be free of them; for they not only destroy his dinner, but they disturb him even in his chamber, so that he is obliged to be watched while he sleeps.'

The captain, who was ready to jump for joy, remembering poor Whittington's hard case, and the cat he had intrusted to his care, told him he had a creature on board his ship that would kill them all.

The king was still more overjoyed than the captain. 'Bring this creature to me,' says he; 'and if she can really perform what you say, I will load your ship with wedges of gold in exchange for her.'

Away flew the captain, while another dinner was providing, to the ship, and taking puss under his arm, returned to the palace in time to see the table covered with rats and mice, and the second dinner in a fair way to meet with the same fate as the first.

The cat, at sight of them, did not wait for bidding, but sprang from the captain's arms, and in a few moments laid the greatest part of the rats and mice dead at her feet, while the rest, in the greatest fright imaginable, scampered away to their holes.

The king, having seen and considered of the wonderful exploits of Mrs. Puss, and being informed she would soon have young ones, which might in time destroy all the rats and mice in the country, bargained with the captain for his whole ship's cargo, and afterwards agreed to give a pro-digious quantity of wedges of gold, of still greater value, for the cat; with which, after taking leave of their majesties, and other great personages belonging to the court, he, with all his ship's company, set sail, with a fair wind for England, and, after a happy voyage, arrived safely in the port of London.

One morning, Mr. Fitzwarren had just entered his counting-house, and was going to seat himself at the desk, when who should arrive but the captain and mate of the merchant-ship, the Unicorn, just arrived from the coast of Barbary, and followed by several men, bringing with them a prodigious quantity of wedges of gold, that had been paid by the King of Barbary in exchange for the merchandize, and also in exchange for Mrs. Puss. Mr. Fitzwarren, the instant he heard the news, ordered Whittington to be called, and having desired him to be seated, said, 'Mr. Whittington, most heartily do I rejoice in the news these gentlemen have brought you; for the captain has sold your cat to the King of Barbary, and brought you in return more riches than I possess in the whole world; and may you long enjoy them!'

Mr. Fitzwarren then desired the men to open the immense treasures they had brought, and added, that Mr. Whittington had now nothing to do but to put it in some place of safety.

Poor Dick could scarce contain himself for joy; he begged his master to take what part of it he pleased, since to his kindness he was indebted for the whole. 'No, no, this wealth is all your own, and justly so,' answered Mr. Fitzwarren, 'and I have no doubt you will use it generously.'

Whittington, however, was too kind-hearted to keep all himself; and, accordingly, made a handsome present to the captain, the mate, and every one of the ship's company, and afterwards to his excellent friend the footman, and the rest of Mr. Fitzwarren's servants, not even excepting crabbed old Cicely.

After this, Mr. Fitzwarren advised him to send for tradespeople, and get himself dressed as became a gentleman, and made him the offer of his house to live in, till he could provide himself with a better.

When Mr. Whittington's face was washed, his hair curled, his hat cocked, and he was dressed in a fashionable suit of clothes, he appeared as handsome and genteel as any young man who visited at Mr. Fitz-warren's; so that Miss Alice, who had formerly thought of him with compassion, now considered him as fit to be her lover; and the more so, no doubt, because Mr. Whittington was constantly thinking what he could do to oblige her, and making her the prettiest presents imaginable.

Mr. Fitzwarren, perceiving their affection for each other, proposed to unite them in marriage, to which, without difficulty, they each consented; and accordingly a day for the wedding was soon fixed and they were attended to church by the lord mayor, the court of aldermen, the sheriffs, and a great number of the wealthiest merchants in London; and the ceremony was succeeded by a most elegant entertainment and splendid ball.

History tells us that the said Mr. Whittington and his lady lived in great splendour and were very happy; that they had several children; that he was sheriff of London in the year 1340, and several times afterwards lord mayor; that in the last year of his mayoralty he entertained King Henry the Fifth, on his return from the battle of Agincourt. And some time afterwards, going with an address from the city on one of his majesty's victories, he received the honour of knighthood.

Sir Richard Whittington constantly fed great numbers of the poor; he built a church and college to it, with a yearly allowance to poor scholars, and near it erected an hospital.

The effigy of Sir Richard Whittington was to be seen, with his cat in his arms, carved in stone, over the archway of the late prison of Newgate, that went across Newgate Street.

## ❖ KITTY'S ❖ REQUEST. ❖

I WISH to have my portrait done,
  I'll sit as good as gold;
Please let it be a handsome one,
  Don't make it look too old.
I've made myself so nice and smart,
  Just tell me when you're ready—
Oh dear! You gave me quite a start!
  There! Silence! Ready! Steady!!

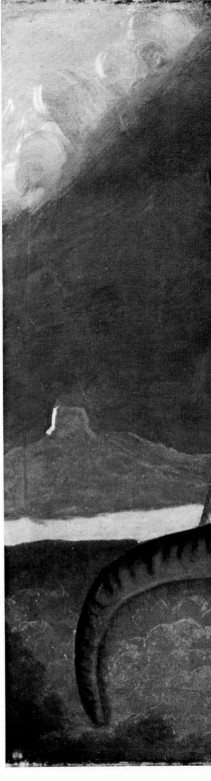

2 Portrait of a white Persian cat called *Psyche* painted by the Elder Sartorius in 1787

3 Study of a mother cat playing with her kittens by the Swiss painter and wood sculptor, Gottfried Mindt (1768–1814) whose fondness for cats as a subject earned him the title 'the Cat Raphael'. A collection of engravings after his work may be found in *Der Katzen-Raphael* published in Berlin in 1861 and another example of his work is shown on page **66** of this book

4 This portrait of two feline friends, one of whom is sleepily toying with a hazel-nut, was done by an anonymous English naive painter in the early 19th century

**5** *Framed*, a portrait of her cat *Simon*, painted in oil on board by Mrs M. Lewis *

**6** Portrait of a young girl with a tabby cat in her arms, done by an unknown English painter at the beginning of the 19th century

**7** Portrait of a kitten painted in watercolour on velvet by a British primitive artist during the 19th century. This picture forms one of a pair, the other painting being a watercolour on velvet of a puppy

**8** Late 19th-century study in oil on canvas of a mother cat and her kittens, signed 'Horatio H. Couldery 1874' and reproduced by courtesy of Miss G. L. Ellis*

5

6

7

8

9

10

11

9 Late 19th-century terracotta statue of a stalking cat by the British-born children's book illustrator, Randolph Caldecott who died in St. Augustine's, Florida in 1886. Other examples of this artist's work may be seen on pages 4–5

10 *Coquetry*, a sentimental picture painted in 1891 by the prolific Dutch-born cat artist, Henriette Ronner-Knip (1821–1909) in her Brussels studio. Here, a gracious mother cat looks on, as her young daughter practices the art of flirtation in a mirror

11 Late 19th-century American trade card in which the cat has been made to assume a rather unfeline 'faithful dog' pose

12

13

12 Portrait of a long-haired tabby cat, painted in oil on board and signed 'Harry Clayton Adams 1899'

13 Early 20th-century watercolour of five striped cats by the humorous British cat artist Louis Wain (1860–1939). A biographical note about Louis Wain is given on page 11 and another unsigned example of his striped cat work is shown on page 63

14 Edwardian watercolour on paper of two tabby kittens wearing blue satin bows, reproduced by courtesy of Mrs J. Davis *

15 Undated primitive painting of unknown origin, but bought in Naples, showing the interior of a stable with a white cat comfortably seated on the back of a miniature pony

16 Cartoon by Sandy Wilson of Laurence Fortescue, the famous feline dramatist, actor and song-writer of the 1920s and 30s. Laurence makes a brief appearance in Sandy Wilson's book *Who Is Sylvia* published by Max Parrish, London in 1954, where he is the friend of a feline musical-comedy star Sylvia Gutts-Whytyng. All the cats in this very amusing book move in the glittering theatrical circle which produced such shows as *The Maid of the Miowntains, Kiss Me Cat, Pussy Be Good, The Tom Boy* and *An Alley-Cat Named Desirée*

14

15

16

*Laurence Fortescue*

**18**

17 Black and white cat painted in oil
on board by the British naive artist
Fred Aris (1934) for whom the cat
is constantly recurring theme

18 Portrait of a little girl with a black
cat in her arms painted in oil on board
by Fred Aris

FIVE CAT PORTRAITS BY CHILDREN

**19** *Catty Cut-Out* painted in watercolour on paper by Karen Staplehurst and mounted on a green background *

**20** *LuLu,* painted in watercolour on paper by Karen Towers and reproduced by courtesy of Mr and Mrs Philip Dalton

**21** *The Ginger Cat Next Door But Two* painted in watercolour on paper by Rosemary Black *

**22** *Mitsi,* painted in watercolour on paper by Nicola Hunter *

**23** *Black Cat* painted in watercolour on paper by Kathleen Armour *

20

19

21

22

23

24

25

26

27

28

**24** Portrait of her cat *Tiger* done in scraperboard by Mrs Janice Hinton *

**25** Portrait of his cat *Timothy* done in scraperboard by Brian William Hall in 1974 *

**26** Portrait of an unsociable cat painted in watercolour on brown paper by Mrs Joan Goode *

**27** White paper sculpture of a cat by the British designer, writer and cat cartoonist Bruce Angrave

**28** Portrait of *Top Kat* drawn in pen and ink by A. M. Morgan in 1973 and reproduced here courtesy of Mrs M. P. Moore *

**30** *Tabitha*, an oil painting in *pointilliste* technique by the leading British naive painter James Lloyd (1905–74)

**31** Portrait of *Tina* painted in oil on board by Max Furst and reproduced by courtesy of Mr and Mrs W. Weinberg*

**32** Portrait of *Sam* painted in oil on board by John Carwithen in 1976 and reproduced by courtesy of Bryan and Angela Tansley *

33

34

35

**33** Head of a British Blue painted in oil on metal by Mrs Eileen Ferguson *

**34** Portrait head of *Snowflake* drawn in pencil on thin card by Dolores Jordan *

**35** *Perceptive Cat* worked in oil pastel on board by Mrs Janet Argent *

**36** *Large Cat* painted in oil on board by Robert McAulay *

37

38

K. J. Widdup.

40

41

39

37 Study of a cat dozing by the fire, painted in oil on paper by Miss Juliet Robson

38 Portrait of *Thomas,* a fourteen-year old cat, drawn in pastel on paper by Miss Margaret Huber *

39 Portrait of *Cattling* reclining against a doorstep, painted in oil on board and reproduced courtesy of Mrs E. Hurst *

40 Portrait of *Duffy,* a white Persian kitten, painted in oil on board by Mrs K. J. Widdup *

41 Portrait head of *Sandy* painted in watercolour on paper by Mr Jack Fisher *

42 Portrait of a cat seated on a kitchen window-sill worked in oil crayon on embossed paper by Miss Carole Pryce *

43

**43** *The Elusive Butterfly* painted in watercolour on paper by Miss Mamie Farms *

**44** Portrait of *Micky Monkers* painted in oil on canvas by Mrs Patricia Hooper *

**45** Portrait of *Trixie* surveying the world from a garden wall painted in oil on canvas and reproduced courtesy of Mrs M. Pluck *

44

45

THE END